I0644247

Why Does It
Have to Hurt?

Why Does It Have to Hurt?

The Meaning of Christian Suffering

Dan G. McCartney

P&R
PUBLISHING
P.O. BOX 817 • PHILLIPSBURG • NEW JERSEY 08865-0817

Unless otherwise indicated, Scripture quotations are from the HOLY BIBLE, NEW INTERNATIONAL VERSION. Copyright © 1973, 1978, 1984 International Bible Society. Used by permission of Zondervan Bible Publishers. Italics indicate emphasis added.

Printed in the United States of America

Library of Congress Cataloging-in-Publication Data

McCartney, Dan.
    Why does it have to hurt? : the meaning of Christian suffering / Dan G. McCartney.
        p.   cm.
    Includes bibliographical references.
    ISBN 0-87552-386-2 (pbk.)
    1. Suffering—Religious aspects—Christianity. I. Title.
BT732.7.M44 1998
231'.8—dc21   97–48594

Contents

A Problem for All Seasons

MY GOD, MY GOD, why have you abandoned me? Why have you abandoned ME!

Jesus cried those words. Have you? I would guess, since you are reading this book, that you have at least once or twice come face to face with the mind-numbing sense that God has not only abandoned you but is actively sending turmoil into your life. If you haven't yet, you will. And if you are relating to God personally and honestly, you too will cry out in confusion from time to time. You will sometimes have questions that seem almost blasphemous to raise.

Why did my father, one of the kindest, most humble, and most gentle men I have ever known, have to endure the horrible prolonged agony of cancer in his bones? Why does my friend, a godly man struggling with cancer, have to endure the added burden of his son's addiction to cocaine? Why was a four-year-old child who was adopted at birth and growing up in a stable home taken from the only parents he has ever known and given to his biological father by some judge, in contradiction of the state's adoption laws? And why did that biological father who pursued this legal travesty then aban-

don the child? Why does God allow extremists who call themselves Christians to blow up buildings with little kids inside?
Why are little kids in the city randomly shot in shoot-outs
between drug dealers? Why does God inflict not just momentary suffering but *generations* of suffering by taking a
mother away from her young children? Why does God permit things like the genocide in Rwanda, the torture and execution of millions of Jews in Germany, the Armenian
massacre in Turkey, the famine and fighting in Somalia, or
the destruction of millions of not-yet-born infants by the in-
jection of salt into their brains, or a host of other horrors?

These questions are hard enough. But it gets even harder
when you, or someone you deeply love, suffers personally.
Then the questions become excruciating. Suffering raises the
deepest questions of life, of meaning, of reality, of truth, of
personhood. It is natural to ask such questions. In fact, it is
unnatural not to ask them. We instinctively recognize that
suffering ought not to be. We know that something is *wrong*.
Suffering is one of the deep, disturbing mysteries of life. Some
mysteries, like why some stars appear older than the universe,
bother astrophysicists but do not touch us. The mystery of
suffering, however, confronts everyone. It is a problem for all
seasons.

Both Christians and non-Christians face this mystery, but
it is a particularly crucial question for Christians, who believe that God is both good and all-powerful. Remember the
command in 1 Peter that you should "be prepared to give an
answer to everyone who asks you to give the reason for the
hope that you have" (3:15)? That command occurs in a passage dealing with suffering! Being always ready to explain
our hope means being able to deal with this problem.

The meaning of suffering is not only important for our
defending Christianity before the world. It is perhaps the
hardest question of all for Christians to answer *for themselves*.

We are psychologically incapable of leaving this question alone. Suffering gets personal. We may ignore it for a while, but as soon as *we* experience suffering, the question comes back as insistently as ever. And when we or someone we love suffers greatly and the world appears senseless and God is as remote as he can be, the question becomes all-consuming. The question "Why?" becomes "Why *me?*" How can *we* make sense out of something that appears so senseless?

Christians must think about these questions. Suffering generates feelings that are often jumbled and incoherent, and to make sense of things and bring order to our feelings, we need truth. And to find truth, we must turn to the Scriptures.

I must say up front that I do not think the Bible gives anything like a definitive answer to every question on suffering. But the Bible does speak of it often; it shows us how to view suffering, and it points to specific ways in which God *uses* suffering.

In fact, we could say that the Bible is *the* book about suffering. From suffering's origins in the Fall of humanity in Genesis 3 to its final defeat in Revelation 21, over and over the biblical writers raise the questions of why God's chosen people are suffering and what their response should be. Israel's bondage in Egypt, Israel's suffering in the wilderness, their experience of oppression from their neighbors, their constant warfare, their droughts, and their exile are all problems for the biblical writers. Indeed, it was the question of suffering that gave rise to most of the Bible. And it is not just the travails of the collective people that are in view. Job's individual, personal afflictions, the psalmists' troubles, and the persecutions of the prophets give cause for questioning God again and again. And the New Testament deals not only with the suffering of God's people but also with the agonizing question of why God's own unique Son suffered.

After almost two thousand years of theological medita-
tion, Christ's suffering does not appear very problematic to
us. But to Christians of the first century, the suffering of the
Messiah was a huge stumbling block. Remember how Peter
reacted when Jesus first said he had to suffer and die? "No
way, Jesus—you can't do that; God would never allow it."
How could God allow his anointed conqueror to be put to
death by Rome—and so ignominiously? The Bible's answers
to suffering are never simple, but they do help us to put our
own sufferings in perspective and to learn to trust God.

This book will focus on certain key passages of Scripture
to answer the "whys" of suffering. First, in answer to the question "Why is there suffering at all?" chapter 1 will look closely
at Genesis 3. After we see how God and suffering are related
(chapter 2), I will focus on how God's sovereignty relates to
this question, first in general (chapter 3) and then with special attention to Job and the problem of *unjust* suffering (chapter 4). Chapters 5 through 8 ask more specifically why
Christians suffer, looking particularly at 1 Peter. Finally, I will
address how we can endure suffering (chapter 9) and examine some psalms that are most helpful to sufferers (chapter
10).

CHAPTER 1

Why Is There Suffering at All?
A Look at Genesis 3

IF YOU BELIEVE IN GOD, you have a problem. If God is both good and all-powerful, how can there be suffering in the world? Why did God permit it in the first place? Could he not have created a perfect world without suffering and death? These are not just abstract questions for theologians—they are questions that deeply trouble us, especially when we ourselves encounter suffering. But before we can answer any of these questions, we must think about what suffering is.

What Is Suffering?

If you are going through suffering, you may think this is a stupid question. But experiencing something, and knowing what it is, are not the same. Suffering is not just pain. Pain is ordinarily a good thing. It keeps the body sound, it trains reflexes and coordination, and it teaches the body what to avoid. Philip Yancey's classic book *Where Is God When It Hurts?*[1] has an extensive chapter on the pain system that shows how excellent it is for the functioning of the body. In fact, when the pain system stops working, as in the case of leprosy (Hansen's disease), it is devastating for the body. If we say, "Well, yes, pain is good, but why does it have to *hurt?*" the answer is that it must hurt or we don't pay enough attention to it. God knew what he was doing when he created a nervous system that feels pain.

In fact, only recently has pain itself been regarded as something we think we should not have to experience. In modern America we think we deserve to be insulated from all pain, even accidental pain or pain caused by our own foolishness, and we press lawsuits for "pain and suffering" even when we ourselves are largely responsible. But for most of the world's history, pain has been regarded simply as a part of life.

Oddly, my own experience with extreme physical pain has not produced the same kinds of questions as those raised by experiencing evil. When I was writhing on a floor five thousand miles from home and screaming my head off, I was not asking "Why?" or any other complicated question. My thought processes could hold onto little more than "God, please make it stop!" I had no ability to reflect on whether God was really there, or whether I was being punished, or how God's sovereignty fit into the picture, or any other theological question. But when I experience suffering because of evil, then all kinds of questions flood in.

Our real problem is not pain but senseless, seemingly arbitrary pain, or pain deliberately caused by others, and above all, *mortal* pain, pain which goes all the way to death. *Oppression,* or wanton infliction of pain both physical and mental by other people or demonic powers, is what is evil. If you look at the word for "suffer" in the New Testament, you will notice it is never used for just pain; suffering always refers to oppression, or something caused by wickedness.[2] In fact, it most often refers to Christ's suffering or the suffering that Christians experience because they belong to Christ. It can be physical, but it can equally well involve being slandered or having family relationships damaged. The Hebrew Old Testament does not have a word that quite matches the Greek word for "suffer." But its more descriptive terms, translated "affliction," "trouble," "oppression," or "grief," which indicate poverty or any humiliating condition, are all very common. These too indicate conditions caused by evil. It is when you experience affliction and oppression, when pain runs amok, when pain is seemingly futile, and when evil is so clearly present, that questions are raised. Then is when you begin to question all you know of God—his wisdom, his justice, his goodness, his sovereignty, even his being.

Another difference between pain and suffering is that pain is experienced by the body and could be good or bad, but suffering is experienced by the *self*, the person, the "soul," the "I." As C. S. Lewis noticed, "You don't merely suffer but have to keep on thinking about the fact that you suffer."[3] Suffering is the soul's response to experiencing evil. If you are suffering, it might be because of the evil of disruption or alienation from your body (physical suffering). But it is more likely that you are feeling a form of alienation from others as the victim of oppression, racism, hatred, or a shattered marriage, or you've experienced betrayal, abandonment, or dehumanization. Or perhaps you are alienated within yourself, experiencing depression, trauma, jealousy, self-hatred, psychosis, hopelessness, or humiliation. And to top it off, perhaps you are feeling abandoned by and separated from God. All of these are your *soul's* experience of evil. Where did all this evil kind of suffering come from?

The Origin of Human Suffering

For Christians, this *appears* to be an easy question. The Bible answers it clearly and early. In fact, it is the first issue addressed after the account of creation. Most readers of this book probably already know the story in Genesis 3, which tells how Adam and Eve tried to declare their independence from God and how human life was cursed as a result. What many people do not realize, however, is that this story of the origin of human suffering contains within it the seeds of God's *remedy* for suffering. The first and most significant curse fell not on people but on the Serpent.

> So the LORD God said to the serpent, "Because you have done this, Cursed are you above all the live-stock and all the wild animals! You will crawl on your belly and you will eat dust all the days of your life. And I will put enmity between you and the woman, and between your offspring and hers; he will crush your head, and you will strike his heel." (vv. 14–15)

This story is not about how the snake developed its means of locomotion; it is about the humiliation and curse of Satan, the great enemy of God and humanity. God was not about to allow humanity to be Satan's tame pet. So God first dealt with the perpetrator of this evil by setting up a war. God is a God of peace, but he does not make peace with Satan. In fact it is *because* God is a God of peace that he is at war, and sets us at war, with Satan. Paul tells the Roman Christians that "the God of peace will soon crush Satan under *your* feet" (Rom. 16:20). God is winning the war, and has even won the war already, because the Man Jesus Christ crushed the head of Satan by his crucifixion and resurrection; yet Christians are getting their feet bloody. Warfare is not at all comfortable—it is the source of vast suffering, even for the victors. Satan is not holding back anything in this war. He hates humanity because it reminds him of God, and so humanity, the "image of God," has become Satan's target for "getting back at" God. But we should also remember that humankind is also a bane to Satan.

Suffering in Relationships

It was not only Satan who was cursed. God also cursed the rebellious man and woman. First, he said to the woman: "I will greatly increase your pains in childbearing; with pain you will give birth to children. Your desire will be for your husband, and he will rule over you" (v. 16).

Here is the origin of suffering by disruption of human relationships. Rather than harmony in marriage, there will be oppression and tyranny. A shadow will pall the joy of procreation by the tremendous pain and danger added to it. Note, by the way, that when the woman is cursed in Genesis 3, God says that he will *greatly increase* the pain in childbearing, which suggests that even before the Fall there was pain. But after our rebellion it became suffering. And perhaps the increased "pain in childbearing" includes not only the physical pain, which is usually over in a few hours, but the agonies of raising children.

Although this curse is directed to the woman, it is actually of broader application than the female half of humanity. The curse on human relationships not only means that marriage will be disharmonious and women will be oppressed; all the relationships of family and people are disrupted. Husbands abuse their wives, and wives manipulate their husbands. The "generation gap" is not unique to our century; parents and children have complained about each other for millennia. And we see right in the next chapter in Genesis how soon sibling rivalry blossomed into fratricide. Perhaps more suffering is generated within families than in any other social arena.

Suffering unto Death

Finally, God curses Adam, who here represents all humans, for his rebellion.

> To Adam he said, "Because you listened to your wife and ate from the tree about which I commanded you, 'You must not eat of it,' Cursed is the ground because of you; through painful toil you will eat of it all the days of your life. It will produce thorns and thistles for you, and you will eat the plants of the field. By the sweat of your brow you will eat your food until you return to the ground, since from it you were taken; for dust you are and to dust you will return." (vv. 17–19)

Some people have observed that God says the ground, not the man, was cursed. Nevertheless, this is certainly a curse on the man, because the point is that all humanity will have a tough life, with death at the end of it. Work, rather than being a delight, became frustrating and unrewarding. Instead of cooperating with humanity, the earth resists yielding its benefits and will throw all kinds of obstacles in the way of enjoyment of work. Even the best of jobs now has its agonies, its setbacks, and its frustrations. Conversely, humankind has become destructive toward the very means of sustenance (the earth), wantonly killing and polluting for short-term economic gain. And of course the ultimate curse is death, the climax of suffering. Until the end of this world, people will die gruesomely. There is no escape.

Suffering and Redemption

The main point of Genesis 3 is this: God has ordained suffering! It is a result of his curse. Suffering is not something outside of his dominion or beyond his control. But also note here that suffering is not merely punitive. It is also *redemptive*. Suffering is not God's vindictive bashing of humanity for its disobedience; it is God's means of restoring rightness to his creation and rescuing us from the evil situation we produced for ourselves.

We can see this from the curses themselves. The curse of the Serpent (which also involves suffering for the offspring of the woman) is sometimes called the "proto-gospel," the first announcement of the Redeemer. The descendant of the woman will crush Satan's head. Warfare with Satan is the first correlate of peace with God. Deliverance from sin and its consequences is going to come by way of those consequences.

Further, Adam and Eve were expelled from the Garden and denied access to the tree of life. The curse condemned them to death. But it turned out that the most redemptive act of all was death, the death of the ultimate Human Being, Jesus Christ. *By taking the curse himself, God transformed the curse into redemption, including the curse that we experience in our own suffering.* We will return to this idea later, but here we should note that if our first parents had been able to eat of that tree and live forever, then there could have been no redeeming death, and they and we would have continued forever in separation from God.

Even the curse of the woman is, according to 1 Timothy 2:15, a conduit of salvation. The enigmatic saying, "She will be saved through the childbearing" does not mean that a woman is spiritually saved by her own physical bearing of children, but that, as she is linked to Eve, womankind is instrumental in salvation by the childbearing, the bringing forth of Jesus, the "seed of the woman" who would crush the head of the Serpent, according to the promise of Genesis 3:15.[4] I think it is also a reminder that women experience a unique kind of pain. It is extremely intense pain (I have heard), but there is joy at the end of it. It reminds us also of another statement of Paul's that "we must through many tribulations enter the kingdom of God" (Acts 14:22 NKJV).

So the general answer to why there is suffering is, oddly, because God *cares* about the relationship he has with his image bearers. He does not shrug off our rebellion. Suffering is part of the curse that results from sin, but suffering is also part of the solution.

Evil and Suffering

But is not suffering evil? Yes, in the sense that evil is at the root of all suffering. Either human wickedness or demonic wickedness lies behind all suffering. Even disease is classifiable as oppression by Satan—it is a bondage (Luke 13:16).

As Peter Kreeft points out,[5] there are three kinds of evil: Sin is our rebellion against and alienation from God. Death is the consequence of sin, alienation from our bodies. Suffering is the consequence of sin that involves alienation and disharmony between ourselves as embodied beings and the rest of creation. Since our bodies are part of the world, suffering is deadly, and death is the ultimate suffering. Sin, death, and suffering separate us from God, our bodies, and the world.

Suffering is evil, because evil is any "breaking of what is good." But if suffering is evil, how can God allow it? There is no complete answer to this question, but we must say at the outset that the Bible tells us God can *use* evil, including suffering, for his own good purposes (Gen. 50:20) even when we cannot know what those purposes may be.

Here is where we must start. God's sovereignty is the most important groundwork for any biblical dealing with suffering. If God does not have control over evil, then evil is only senseless and meaningless, and it is silly to ask, "Why is there suffering?" I will say more on this later. But in answer to the general question, "Why is there suffering?", the answer is that *suffering is always a consequence of the curse*. It is therefore *indirectly* the consequence of our sinfulness.

Now, suffering is *sometimes* the direct consequence of our own sin (Jer. 13:22). This only makes sense. If we attempt to "violate" God's physical laws (such as gravity), we suffer the consequences. So it should not be surprising to discover that violating God's moral laws also results in evil consequences, to ourselves and others. Our society encourages us to slough off responsibility, and there is a danger that we may blind ourselves to our own sin as the cause of our suffering.

On the other hand, in this life the *direct* cause of suffering may be, in fact probably more often is, the sin of someone else, or even of no one in particular. Clearly, the people who suffered in the Oklahoma City bombing were not suffering for their own sins; they were and are suffering because of someone else's sin. There is often very little correlation between a particular instance of suffering and an identifiable sin on the part of the sufferer.

But our *susceptibility* to suffering, and the ultimate causes for the imposition of suffering in general, lie in humanity's Great Rebellion. Jesus pointed out (Luke 13:1–5) that the Galileans whom Pilate had wantonly murdered did not suffer because they were especially wicked; they suffered because suffering is the lot of fallen humankind.

> Do you think that these Galileans were worse sinners than all the other Galileans because they suffered this way? I tell you, no! But unless you repent, you too

> will all perish. Or those eighteen who died when the
> tower in Siloam fell on them—do you think they were
> more guilty than all the others living in Jerusalem? I
> tell you, no! But unless you repent, you too will all
> perish. (vv. 2–5)

Suffering tells us that something is wrong. If there were
no suffering, how many of us would be concerned either
with God or with the welfare of others? The overwhelming immensity of suffering, the fact that there is *so much*
of it, ought to give us some indication of the magnitude of
the wrongness in the world and the enormity of humanity's sinfulness.

If we return now to our earlier question, "Why did God
allow sin in the first place?", although we cannot give a definitive and total answer, we can say a few things. Paul tells
us that God allowed sin because the process of redeeming
people from sin would bring greater honor, a kind of aston-
ishment at the extent of God's grace (see for example Rom.
5:20). Also, as the theologians of the Middle Ages used to
point out, the unity of Christians with their God in the God-
Man Jesus Christ was in a way the result of humankind's sin.
But even with these "answers" we cannot fully know why
God should allow sin in his universe. We can only thank
him that he has overcome it.

Suffering by itself, however, is not the severest question
we face. More crucial is the question, Why is there *unjust*
suffering? We will turn to this question in the next chapter.

For Further Reflection

1. Have you experienced deep suffering? What for you has
   raised the most serious questions in your life? How did
   you handle it?

2. Do you agree that "if you believe in God, you have a problem"? Explain.
3. What is the difference between pain and suffering? Is mental illness or psychological depression a form of suffering?
4. Comment on the idea that suffering is a result of our sinfulness, but not necessarily a result of our own sin?
5. How can you tell if your suffering is directly the result of your own sin?
6. Is all suffering evil? Explain.
7. "Suffering tells us that something is wrong." How? Can we benefit from knowing that?

NOTES

1. New York: Harper, 1977.
2. The only possible exception may be the woman suffering with a long-term hemorrhage in Mark 5:25–26, but even here it could be that the suffering was from the *physicians* who took advantage of her distress and bled her of all her money. Further, as Jesus indicates in Luke 13:16, physical ailments are a form of oppression by Satan. Jesus' healings, as well as his exorcisms, were a sign of his victory over Satan.
3. C. S. Lewis, *A Grief Observed* (New York: Seabury, 1961), 12.
4. Cf. G. W. Knight, *The Pastoral Epistles: A Commentary on the Greek Text* (Grand Rapids: Eerdmans, 1992), 146f.
5. P. Kreeft, *Making Sense of Suffering* (Ann Arbor: Servant Press, 1986), 24.

CHAPTER 2

Suffering and God

THE BIBLE CLAIMS that God is good, loving, kind, and merciful. God hates evil. Further, the Bible claims that God is omnipotent (that is, he is *able* to do whatever he pleases) and that he exercises total sovereignty (that is, he *does* whatever he pleases). He is therefore able to eliminate evil and suffering, and yet there is evil and suffering in the world. This appears to be a contradiction, does it not?

The forensic anthropologist Douglas Ubelaker relates a story[1] about a young woman who in 1977 was abducted, raped, and shot only a week before she was to be married. After about six months, the killer brought the girl's head in a plastic bag to the police, saying he had a dream about the murder. After some pointed questioning by the police he confessed, and other evidence also confirmed that he was the killer. But later, he changed his story and pleaded innocent. Florida law only allows confessions as evidence if it can be proved that the death was caused by criminal agency or resulted from a criminal act. In spite of the bullet hole in her skull, Judge William Rowley decided the evidence of criminal agency was inadequate and threw the case out. The murderer walked free and cannot be re-tried. What would you have said to the young woman's fiancé, who witnessed this juridical fiasco? How would you convince him that God is all-powerful, just, and good?

The problem can be put even more sharply. We shudder at Auschwitz precisely because it was a *deliberate* act. How could people (the Nazis were, after all, people) deliberately inflict such unbelievable suffering upon millions of people, including little children? But for the Christian who believes in God's sovereignty, this problem is a thousand times greater. How could God *deliberately* inflict suffering upon *billions* of people, including little children? By not acting when he could, he is at least deliberately allowing it. And sometimes it even appears that he is conspiring it.

In October of 1990, a ten-year-old girl named Charity went to a roller-skating rink about five miles from home with her friends. Her mother had gone out for the evening and hired a baby-sitter to watch her two younger children. Charity was supposed to call the baby-sitter when the rink closed so that she could come and pick her up. When the rink closed, her friends were picked up by their father. A half-hour later she walked to a nearby Hardees and asked what time it was. At about 1:00 A.M. the person closing up Hardees noticed her sitting out on the curb. It was the last anyone acknowledges seeing her alive. Her body was found a few days later—she had been raped and strangled. Why didn't Charity call home? It turned out that Charity's younger brothers and sisters had been playing and had knocked the phone off the hook, and the baby-sitter never noticed it. After the children were in bed, the baby-sitter fell asleep, and it was not until Charity's mother came home that anyone realized anything was wrong.[2]

When I first read that story, it actually produced a little crisis of faith for me. What could God's interest possibly be in ordaining a whole series of events to produce exactly the sequence that resulted in this tragedy? If the kids had not knocked the phone off, or if the baby-sitter had not fallen asleep, or if Charity's friends had given her a ride home, or if her mother had come home a bit earlier, or if a murdering rapist had not been in the vicinity at just that time, then this horrible evil would never have befallen her. Is God some kind of cosmic sadist, conspiring against this little ten-year-old girl to ensure her suffering and death?

Is God All-powerful?

One way of solving the problem is to deny that God is all-powerful. Many people have taken this approach, but perhaps the most well known is Rabbi Kushner in his book, *When Bad Things Happen to Good People*.[3] In attempting to deal with the death of his son, Kushner concluded that God is actually unable to fix things. According to Kushner, God's importance to us is that he is a friend who feels with us, who provides a focus for our deepest longings and comforts us in our deepest despair. "Bad things happen to good people" because that is the way the world is. God is not responsible for our suffering; rather he is a friend who stands with us in our suffering.

Kushner comes up with some rather odd interpretations of the Bible to support his view. For example, God's words to Job in Job 40–41 are not seen as an expression of God's sovereignty; rather, God is telling Job that he has a tough time running the world and that he cannot always keep bad things from happening chaotically. Kushner says, "To try to explain the Holocaust, or any suffering, as God's will is to side with the executioner rather than with his victim, and to claim that God does the same."[4]

Rabbi Kushner's particular solution is flawed by his question, of course. Many Christians have pointed out that the real question ought not to be "Why do bad things happen to

good people?" but "Why do good things happen to bad people?" This sounds orthodox, but I do not think that kind of
glib response would have satisfied Job. Furthermore, there
was *one* good person, and he suffered more than anybody else.
And even among us sinners the distribution of suffering appears terribly uneven—some very evil people suffer very little in this life, while the kind and gentle and godly often
suffer a great deal. Recognizing the flaw in Rabbi Kushner's
question will not make the problem go away.

Kushner's book has sold millions. Clearly he has touched
a nerve, and his own experience of his son's death gives him
a credibility toward which people gravitate. Why is his book
so popular? I think it is because it provides a kind of solution
to the problem that everyone who believes in God in some
way feels. God can be a friend without being in any way responsible for our suffering, either by action or by inaction.
Kushner's God is accessible, lovable, friendly—a god to whom
we can relate as someone who shares our predicament of suffering and powerlessness. In his system, prayer does not change
things; it only changes *us*. Religion makes us sensitive to other
people's pain and gives us the strength to get through the
suffering by affirming our self-worth.

Certainly it is true that prayer makes us sensitive to other
people and gives us strength, but this god is not the God we
see in the Bible. What good is a God who cannot do anything but wring his hands and sympathize? We do not pray
to our powerless neighbors, be they ever so sympathetic. The
biblical writers prayed to a sovereign who *can* remedy the
situation. Even Jesus in his agony prayed to God, knowing
that the issue was not one of God's power, but of his will:
"Yet not as I will, but as you will."

Rabbi Kushner is not the only one who has tried to deal
with the problem of suffering by making God less than omnipotent. Within the Christian tradition Douglas John Hall

quite self-consciously redefines God.[5] In fact, the "orthodox" God who is all-powerful is repugnant to Hall because to him it would mean that God is an incredibly monstrous deity, cruelly and arbitrarily imposing ghastly tortures upon his helpless creatures. God is not the all-powerful one; he is the one who suffers. Hall has something of an advantage over Kushner because Hall can point to Jesus on the cross and say, "God knows what it is like to suffer—he has himself suffered, and thus can identify with us," which is of course true, and which is a great comfort to Christians. Also unlike Kushner, Hall tries to take human sin seriously. But once again, the powerless god is not the God of the Bible. The biblical writers, even when they are mystified by why God *does* not give relief, always remain full of confidence that God *can* give relief.

Is God Good?

A second way to solve the dilemma is to deny God's goodness. This is what the Gnostics did in the second century. They thought the Creator of this world was evil. According to them, the God of salvation was different from the Creator God. But the Bible is shot through with the assumption of the Creator's goodness. Deuteronomy 32:4 is just one text among many. And just raising the question as to whether God "measures up" to our standard of goodness is to assume that *we* set the standard for goodness, not God. If our standard for goodness is not God himself, then that standard must be in us, in which case there is in fact no *standard* at all, and "goodness" is a meaningless term.

Is Suffering Real?

The third option is to deny that suffering exists. This is the Christian Science approach. Suffering is only an illusion to be conquered by replacing the illusion of suffering with the "reality" of nonsuffering.

Fortunately, few people have such powerful imaginations that they can pretend there is no suffering. Further, Christian Scientists become sick and die just like everyone else. And, if we are having an illusion of suffering, are we not still *suffering* from the illusion?

This approach creates horrible pressures on people who are actually suffering. It makes them feel guilty that they don't have adequate faith to "recognize" that they are not suffering. Further, it allows those who are not suffering to feel good about themselves while having no compassion for those who are suffering. Christian Scientism appeals to the wealthy and healthy. This perverse religion allows people to slough off any sense of responsibility for the poor, with the conviction that those who are suffering are simply ignorant. In short, "He jests at scars that never felt a wound."

A more refined variation on this approach, which is more likely to appeal to genuine Christians, is to redefine suffering as simply a failure to acquiesce to whatever comes our way. Suffering is thus a function of mental attitude. This approach has some appeal because it has a measure of truth—suffering is indeed largely a mental thing. Severe depression is a terrible form of suffering, and often it is not related to any obvious external source. But to make suffering *only* a matter of mental attitude denies the reality of evil.

The ultimate form of this approach is Buddhism, which declares that suffering is nothing more than the gap between what I have and what I want. To get rid of suffering you get rid of all desire (including the desire to be free of pain). Nirvana, the end of suffering, is the extinction of all desire. Peter Kreeft points out that this is like killing the patient in order to cure the disease, a kind of spiritual euthanasia.[6] Further, this approach completely isolates God from this world, and God simply becomes an intellectual thing, having nothing to do with the world we actually live in.

If we take any of these routes, then we have a god who is not really the God of the Bible. So, the argument goes, the existence of evil disproves the biblical God. But we would point out that no alternative to Christianity has any *answer* to suffering or any way to explain our sense of the wrongness of it. Without God, suffering is simply there; it does not *mean* anything, and its wrongness is no more than a matter of dislike.

Suffering and Meaning

Perhaps few books convey more vividly the awfulness of evil in our century than Elie Wiesel's *Night*.[7] The book simply tells a story. But the story raises intensely the human problem: on the one hand the specter of evil is seldom seen so clearly; and on the other, every ground for supposing that good and evil are meaningful is removed. Wiesel relates how his soul was destroyed at his first night in concentration camp:

> Never shall I forget that night, the first night in camp, which has turned my life into one long night, seven times cursed and seven times sealed. Never shall I forget that smoke. Never shall I forget the little faces of the children, whose bodies I saw turned into wreaths of smoke beneath a silent blue sky.
>
> Never shall I forget those flames which consumed my faith forever.
>
> Never shall I forget that nocturnal silence which deprived me, for all eternity, of the desire to live. Never shall I forget those moments which murdered my God and my soul and turned my dreams to dust. Never shall I forget these things, even if I am condemned to live as long as God Himself. Never.[8]

Wiesel was fifteen years old. Sometime later, after seeing a child hanged slowly, he heard someone in the camp asking, "Where is God now?" Wiesel says, "I heard a voice within me answer him: 'Where is He? Here He is—He is hanging here on this gallows. . . .' "9

There is obviously a great deal of evil in the world. Yet apart from the fact that it is emotionally shocking and makes us uncomfortable, what reason could Elie Wiesel give to suggest that what the Nazis did was wrong? Only the belief in a divinely ordered morality, which he rejected in the face of the moral horrors he encountered, can provide a basis for declaring such behavior as absolutely evil, and without such belief the word "evil" has no real meaning. It is just a term referring to something I dislike.

God and Meaning

On the other hand, the existence of suffering and evil, although a huge problem, does mean something if we acknowledge God. The question "Why is there suffering?" assumes that God exists and that suffering has meaning. When something has meaning, it serves as a pointer to something else. If suffering *means* something, then we must look beyond the suffering itself to a Personal One who gives it meaning. Without God, the question "Why is there suffering?" is pointless because there can be no "why" to suffering or any other evil. Humans instinctively ask "why," because they instinctively know that the sovereign God is supposed to be good. When we stop asking why, to some degree our humanity dies. François Mauriac, in the preface to Wiesel's *Night*, describes Wiesel's countenance many years later:

> . . . that look, as of a Lazarus risen from the dead, yet still a prisoner within the grim confines where he had

strayed, stumbling among the shameful corpses. For him Nietzsche's cry expressed an almost physical reality: God is dead, the God of love, of gentleness, of comfort, the God of Abraham, of Isaac, of Jacob, has vanished forevermore, beneath the gaze of this child, in the smoke of a human holocaust exacted by Race, the most voracious of all idols.[10]

Wiesel could no longer believe in a sovereign God, or at least no longer in a good one. But if there is no sovereign God, then our existence and deeds are all simply the product of blind chance, and there can be no such thing as morality except in an empty, functionalistic sense, and if our Creator is not morally good, then our differentiation between good and evil is purely a figment of our own imaginings or an expression of personal taste. Our recognition that some things are *evil* and not just unpleasant is *prima facie* evidence within our own consciousness that there is a standard of morality outside of ourselves that exists because a moral God made us.

Only those with an extremely powerful imagination can succeed in denying that there is evil in the world, and even those people who do are rarely consistent in denying it. It may be possible to claim that *pain* is amoral; but as soon as one says that the Holocaust was *wrong*, the universe is assumed to be moral, and a moral Creator has tacitly been assumed. The way out for a lot of people today who want to deny such a Creator is to say that there is no *absolute* wrong or right, since nothing governs the whole universe always, or that morality is a function of humanity as a whole. But then we ask the question, Was Hitler's "final solution" *absolutely* wrong? People know in their guts that certain things are *wrong*, which shows that they know in their guts that there is a moral Creator.

I have never experienced the kind of horror that fifteen-year-old Elie Wiesel did, and therefore much of what I have said will seem empty to some people. But there were other people who endured similar and even worse horrors, without the same effect. I know another Jewish man who was also interned in a concentration camp, who saw untold horrors and only barely escaped extermination. He had a long road of psychological recovery, and to this day he cannot easily discuss it, but he later bowed to the sovereignty of God and clasped his suffering Son as his only answer. Is it not a sad irony that Elie Wiesel thought he saw God hanging on a gallows, but he has failed to look at the God who did indeed hang on a gallows for our sake?

For Further Reflection

1. What are the three ways people have tried to deal with the problem of suffering and God's sovereignty? Can you think of others besides these?
2. How does Rabbi Kushner's explanation of God's relationship to suffering compare with the Bible's? Why do you think people are attracted to Kushner's solution to the problem?
3. Have you ever had a crisis of faith over your own or someone else's suffering? Do you think we ought to try to suppress our doubts?
4. Have you ever felt like Elie Wiesel? Does a Christian have anything to say to Elie Wiesel that would not sound trite in his ears?
5. Can the existence of evil be a proof *for* God's existence? How so?

NOTES
1. The story is recounted in D. Ubelaker, *Bones: A Forensic Detective's Casebook* (New York: Harper, 1992), 124–27.

2. Ibid., 117–18.
3. Harold S. Kushner, *When Bad Things Happen to Good People* (New York: Avon, 1983).
4. Ibid., 82.
5. Douglas John Hall, *God and Human Suffering: An Exercise in the Theology of the Cross* (Minneapolis: Augsburg, 1986).
6. P. Kreeft, *Making Sense of Suffering* (Ann Arbor: Servant Press, 1986), 4.
7. Elie Wiesel, *Night* (New York: Hill & Wang, 1960).
8. Ibid., 43–44.
9. Ibid., 71.
10. F. Mauriac, "Introduction," in Wiesel, *Night*, 9.

CHAPTER 3

God's Sovereignty

IF WE CANNOT DENY God's omnipotence, and we cannot deny his goodness, and we cannot deny that suffering is real, is there any solution to this problem of suffering and evil? The only option that really works leaves mystery. The biblical option is that God indeed is totally sovereign—and he *uses* evil for some good purpose, although many times that purpose is not revealed to us. The mystery is not simply silence, however. The Bible sees a meaning to the mystery in the crucifixion of Jesus. I will come back to this subject later. But at this point it is most crucial that we get this issue of God's sovereignty under our belts.

A Middle Way?

It is not too hard to see what is wrong with Rabbi Kushner's solution, especially for Christians who read the Bible. So several Christians have tried to solve the problem of suffering, not by denying, but by limiting God's sovereignty. On this view, God has the ability to act but refrains from acting. They say God must allow for human freedom, and this means he must allow things to happen outside his control, including sin. God "permits" suffering because he will not barge in and put an end to suffering if it means destroying our freedom. Thus God's sovereignty is re-defined: God has the raw *power* to set everything to rights, but he withholds his power in order not to destroy the free will of his moral creatures. And to destroy the free will would be a greater evil than the evil that those free agents commit.

This has an element of truth to it. It is true that God does not directly cause sin, but he allows it. And God *could* eliminate evil simply by destroying the freedom of his creatures, but he refrains from doing this. Would you prefer it if God did eliminate evil by destroying freedom? I must admit that at times I might have said yes. When you are hurting, delivery from the hurting becomes an exceedingly high priority.

An early episode of Star Trek entitled "Menagerie" involved a paralyzed Captain Pike who was faced with a choice between, on the one hand, the lifetime illusion of health and well being, and, on the other, a lifetime of facing the true situation of paralysis and helplessness. In the story as originally written, Captain Pike eventually turns down the offer of the illusion and sticks with reality. But the version that finally aired has him choose the dream world without even so much as a passing thought for reality and truth. Although many modern sympathies seem to be strongly on the side of anesthesia rather than reality, for strong-souled human beings the loss of truth is itself a form of suffering of the worst kind, and thus the elimination of freedom would really not solve anything. It would simply substitute one kind of suffering for another. So it is indeed important that God preserve our ability to act freely, which allows for evil.

The problem is that not all suffering is due to an expression of human freedom. In New York City four young girls on their way to church school were crushed to a bloody pulp when a gust of wind blew an old tree over on the van they were riding in.[1] No free will lay behind this awful tragedy— it was simply a one-in-a-million fluke accident! Further, if God "must" allow free will, and thus suffering, why do so many psalm authors cry out to God expecting him to *do* something? If God is going to withhold his power so as not to interfere with the free will of the oppressor, why do the biblical writers bother to ask God to deliver them from the oppressor's hand? If they reaffirm their trust in God by the end of the psalm, it is not because they've come to terms with the fact that God does not help the needy; it is because they acknowledge God's greater wisdom.

All Christians know that the Bible expects God to set things right finally, when he judges the world. But will not that great day be "interfering" with the free will of the wicked? Is it evil to pass laws against murder that "restrict" the free will of would-be murderers or to catch and punish such evildoers? It is certainly clear that God refrains from preventing all evil—who knows how much evil he *does* prevent, which we never know about?—but we cannot appeal to the preservation of free will as his reason for doing so. He must have his own purposes.

Prayer and God's Sovereignty

The novelist Peter deVries wrote a very moving story about loss of faith entitled *The Blood of the Lamb*.[2] He puts it pointedly: to *pray* to God for healing implies his sovereignty, and thus the suffering must be within his sovereign disposition. But to Don Wanderhope, the hero of deVries's story, (and presumably to deVries himself) this is intolerable. In the story, Don says to his girlfriend Rena, who is dying of tuberculosis,

> I simply mean that asking Him to cure you—or me,
> or anybody—implies a personal being who arbitrarily
> does us this dirt. The prayer then is a plea to have a
> heart. To knock it off. I find the thought repulsive. I
> prefer to think we're victims of chance to dignifying
> any such force with the name of Providence."[3]

Even though the thought is "repulsive" to Don, it is inescapable. Don is not wrong to suppose that, if God can heal,
then he must also send, or at least allow, suffering. Sadly,
Don cannot see any greater purpose or higher good than his
own comfort and therefore thinks of such suffering as arbitrary and cruel. But he recognizes that unless God has sovereign control over suffering, it is completely pointless to pray
about it.

Confusion on this point has led to much misunderstand-
ing by Christians on what is involved in asking God for heal-
ing. Don Carson argues that the failure of Christians to reckon
with God's sovereignty in suffering is perhaps a root of the
"signs and wonders" movement in Christianity.[4] These en-
thusiastic Christians *rightly* insist on seeing God's power displayed by his vanquishing sickness, which we see in the
Gospels. Disease *is* a work of the Devil, and God through
Jesus does destroy the works of the Devil, including disease.
But what is sometimes lacking is a proper appreciation of the
fact that God is as powerfully behind the sickness as he is the
source of health. God's hedge is around us to keep Satan from
us (Job 1:10), and if God removes that hedge, he does so for
some good reason. If we do not recognize God's sovereignty
in suffering, then suffering becomes an evil untempered by
any good purpose. Either God has not yet dealt with it (con-
trary to the gospel), or else he is prevented from dealing with
it by our lack of faith (which places a huge load of guilt upon
the sufferer, in much the same way as Job's friends tried to

lay a guilt trip on him). But when you recognize God's sovereignty in suffering as well as in health, it ought to transform your understanding of suffering into something that, while tragic, is also purposeful, an evil that is somehow necessary for our good (Rom. 8:28). As one of the Puritans once observed, "All that he sends is needful; all that is needful he sends."

How can God call himself my shield and fortress if he will not or cannot protect me against humans or devils who by their own free will wish to injure me and my family? If you think that Satan can make you suffer when God has not allowed it, then you can no longer trust God. How can Paul say, "My God will meet all your needs" (Phil 4:19), if in fact he will not, if it means interfering with someone's "free will"? How can your suffering have *any* purpose other than Satan's, which is to defeat you? To trust God is to say you believe he knows what he is doing. But if God is not deliberately *allowing* your suffering, then there can be no meaning to it for you or for anyone, and we might as well quit talking about it. But the Bible doesn't quit talking about it—it finds all kinds of purpose and meaning in suffering, because the biblical writers pray vigorously and have no doubts about God being in control.

The Bible and God's Sovereignty over Evil

The biblical writers are very honest, and when they are confronted with suffering, they may for a while question various attributes of God. They doubt, like Job, whether God is really just. They complain, like Jeremiah, that God has deceived them. They wonder, like the psalmist, if God has abandoned them. But the one attribute that the biblical writers never question is God's power. They never "tone down" God's sovereignty in order to make him "nice," the way Rabbi Kushner and some Christians try to do. Just look at some of the passages that assume God's control of everything, even evil and suffering.

- Proverbs 16:9: "In his heart a man plans his course, but the LORD determines his steps." This Bible writer clearly does not think that man's free will in any way limits God's determination of things.
- Isaiah 45:7: "I form the light and create darkness; I bring prosperity and create disaster; I the LORD do all these things." The Lord *creates* disaster. He is certainly not flabbergasted by it.
- Psalm 60:3: "Thou hast made thy people suffer hard things; thou hast given us wine to drink that made us reel" (RSV). The psalmist understands God as the source of the suffering. Suffering is not outside God's intention.
- Exodus 4:11: God rhetorically asks Moses, "Who gave man his mouth . . . who makes him deaf or mute . . . who gives him sight or makes him blind?" God *makes people deaf and blind!* Not for their sin, or for any identifiable reason necessarily. When Jesus healed the blind man in John 9, he told his disciples that the blindness was due neither to his sin nor to his parents' sin, but simply "so that the work of God might be displayed in his life." Usually we do not even know this much about why someone is born blind; but the point here is that there *was* a purpose to his blindness, and it was *God's* purpose. It was not just "bad luck."
- Acts 4:27–28: The disciples pray, "Indeed Herod and Pontius Pilate met together with the Gentiles and the people of Israel in this city to conspire against your holy servant Jesus, whom you anointed. They did what your power and will had decided beforehand should happen."

The disciples believed that God had planned that the greatest crime in history would be carried out. Herod, Pilate, and the Sanhedrin conspired, but they did so all according to the set purpose of God, who actually drew them together for that very purpose.

But if God really is totally in control, how can we then avoid the charge of Rabbi Kushner that such a God is siding with the executioner or DeVries' complaint that such a God "arbitrarily does us this dirt"?

Although we cannot get rid of the mystery here, since God keeps his own counsel much of the time, we can point out several things. First, at least *some* suffering has a good result that we can sometimes (later) identify. "You meant it for evil but God meant it for good," Joseph tells his brothers who have finally repented of selling him into slavery. Although we cannot *see* the point of *all* suffering (perhaps not even of most suffering), this does not mean that it is arbitrary, or cruel. To claim that God is arbitrary or cruel is to claim to be able to see to the bottom of things, to be omniscient.

Second, remember that the word "evil" can be used in two different ways: it can mean suffering, pain, adversity, calamity, etc., or it can refer to the malice and wickedness of a person who perpetrates such things. Jeremiah 11:17 uses the word in both senses: "The LORD of hosts, who planted you, has pronounced *evil* against you, because of the *evil* which the house of Israel and the house of Judah have done, provoking me to anger by burning incense to Ba'al" (RSV). Obviously the first sort of "evil" is different from the second.

Third, it is also important to realize that, even though God does deliberately allow suffering to occur for his own reasons, such suffering does not leave him unmoved, any more than parents who must hurt their child to deal with a malady are unmoved. Psalm 56:8 says to God, "You have kept count of my tossings; put my tears in your bottle. Are they not in your record?" (NRSV). God keeps track of every one of his children's sorrows, even when he has ordained those sorrows. Just after Jesus utters his most excoriating denunciation of the Jewish leadership for its wickedness, and just before he predicts the city's ignominious future, he weeps for Jerusalem in very moving language.

> O Jerusalem, Jerusalem, you who kill the prophets and stone those sent to you, how often I have longed to gather your children together, as a hen gathers her chicks under her wings, but you were not willing. Look, your house is left to you desolate. (Matt. 23:37–38)

In just a few years a horrible judgment was going to fall upon Jerusalem. But even though God intended for this judgment to fall, it was very grievous to him.

Fourth, God himself has in his Son borne our griefs and carried our sorrows. First Peter 2:24 clearly applies the language of Isaiah 53 to Christ's work on the cross: "He himself bore our sins in his body on the tree, so that we might die to sins and live for righteousness; by his wounds you have been healed."

Again, this theme is surrounded in mystery. God does not just sympathize from a distance; he has himself taken human suffering upon himself to a degree that we cannot begin to understand. The mystery of unjust suffering is compounded by the greater mystery of why God should purpose suffering for his own beloved Son. Even though we know the biblical doctrine, that the suffering and death of Jesus was necessary to remove the wrath that stood against us, the thought of God subjecting his most beloved Son to that wrath in lieu of the persons who deserved it is something we cannot fathom. It makes no sense to us. Somehow it does make sense to God, and we had better be grateful it does. God's purposes are often mysterious, but they are nevertheless *purposes*, not random acts of violence that God is powerless or unwilling to prevent. God suffered not because he was powerless but because he intended to suffer. Jesus said, "I lay down my life for the sheep. . . . *No one takes it from me, but I lay it down of my own accord*" (John 10:15, 18). Thus does suffering have meaning, because it is *not* accidental or arbitrary.

Suffering Is Nothing New

I suppose that everyone who has suffered is tempted to see his or her own suffering as raising questions much more difficult than the suffering of others. We each think we have a corner on suffering. Certainly this century has seen incredible suffering and atrocity. But suffering and atrocity is not unique to this century.

Stanley Hauerwas finds the suffering and death of children to be the hardest existential problem for Christians to deal with in faith. He says this is so because children do not yet have a life story that can give suffering meaning.[5] It all becomes pointless. But although experiencing the death of your *own* child is absolutely devastating, the death of children is not unique to the twentieth century—in fact it used to be much more common. Only nine of J. S. Bach's twenty children survived him. He had to bury *eleven* of his kids. Also, his first wife sickened and died suddenly while Bach was on a brief excursion. When he returned home, he found she had already been buried. Surely, Bach asked many times, "Why, God?" Perhaps the reason Bach could so passionately express in music the suffering of Christ in the St. Matthew Passion was that he knew what suffering was and as a result clung all the more tightly to the only One who made it meaningful, who had himself suffered the death of his own Son.

Further, suffering cannot really be quantified, as J. C. Beker, another survivor of a concentration camp, has written.[6] Does the man who must watch his wife die a prolonged and agonizing death from cancer suffer less than the man who watched his wife be sent to the gas ovens at Auschwitz? Perhaps the latter is harder to accept because it is a deliberate act of vicious people, and it is hard to accept that people can be that bad, but the people who must endure the loss endure the loss in both cases.

Certainly the biblical writers knew suffering. And it is instructive how they respond to it. Psalm 11:3 expresses the devastation that the psalmist feels at God's failure to intervene at the "right time." "When the foundations are being destroyed, what can the righteous do?" When God allows you to undergo suffering, does it not seem that the very foundations of your life, of your faith, are being destroyed? The psalmist's answer is simply to refer to God's sovereign control: "The Lord is in his holy temple; the Lord is on his heavenly throne" (v. 4). In other words, God is in charge, and knows what he is doing. Who knows how long it took the psalmist to work through his suffering to the point of his affirmation? Yet it is the only path worth taking. Every other path leads to emptiness.

For Further Reflection

1. Do you truly believe in God's total sovereignty? Have you found your belief threatened during times of suffering?
2. Evaluate this statement: "I sure didn't need to get sick at this point in my life."
3. How would you talk about the good God's sovereignty (or the sovereign God's goodness) to someone who is now suffering?

4. What is the "middle way" that many Christians adopt in response to Rabbi Kushner's view that God is not all-powerful? Is there an element of truth in this middle way?

5. Though God's control over suffering is largely a mystery beyond our understanding, is there any evidence that even when we are suffering, God loves us, sympathizes with us, and is concerned for our good?

6. If you have experienced suffering, did you believe then that God knew what he was doing? Did that knowledge help?

NOTES

1. *New York Times*, March 7, 1997, A1.
2. Peter deVries, *The Blood of the Lamb* (Boston: Little, Brown & Co., 1969).
3. Ibid., 104.
4. D. A. Carson, *How Long O Lord* (Grand Rapids: Baker, 1990), 123–26.
5. S. Hauerwas, *Naming the Silences* (Grand Rapids: Eerdmans, 1990), 67.
6. Jan Christiaan Beker, *Suffering and Hope: The Biblical Vision and the Human Predicament* (Grand Rapids: Eerdmans, 1987), ix.

Chapter 4

The Lessons of Job

THE BOOK OF JOB vividly shows a man on the path of suffering. If you have been on that path, you know it is not an easy one. But let us follow Job's path for a bit to see what we can learn from this man's experience.

First, let me point out that "wisdom" in the Ancient Near East generally held that there was a direct and observable connection between a person's suffering and some behavior disapproved of by God (or gods). If someone was suffering, it was because he or she had offended some god.

The Bible (especially Proverbs) recognizes that indeed sin against God does often result in suffering as a consequence, but it also recognizes that much suffering cannot be explained that way. In this regard, the Bible, especially the book of Job, stands like a beacon in the ancient world. Rather than being a sign of *disfavor* with God, Job's suffering stood as a sign of God's *favor* and approval. We can read in Job 1 of how God was showing forth the character of Job by allowing Satan's persecutions. But Job himself had no idea why he was suffering.

The First Lesson of Job: We Are Not Wise

God permits suffering for his own glory and our good, but we cannot know the specific reason why he allows it in every instance. If Job teaches us anything, it certainly teaches us that all the various answers to the problem of suffering are inadequate. Some answers may be true some of the time, but there is no definitive answer available to us.[1] Job at first thought he *ought* to be able to understand his suffering. He thought God owed him an explanation. He was wrong. Job's friends thought they really did understand. They were even more wrong. If you are in the place of Job, as the sufferer, you cannot always understand your suffering because you do not know God's purposes. And if you have a friend who is suffering, take care that your good intentions do not turn you into a "Job's friend" and add to your friend's suffering.

It is amazing how common is the view that tragedy must be due to some sin or failure in a person's life. Perhaps because most of us as children experienced very little suffering except when our parents disciplined us for some wrongdoing, we naturally suppose that when evil befalls us, God is punishing us for something.

Shortly after the bombing of the Federal Building in Oklahoma City, I heard an interview with a child psychologist who was discussing the kinds of mental trauma the children would experience. If a child had argued with her mother that morning over eating her cereal, for example, she may feel that the bombing happened as punishment for her disobedience. Adults, too, are adept at blaming themselves for things that are not their fault when bad things happen. Even worse, people often try to tell others who have experienced tragedy that "the Lord must be trying to punish you for something." The friends of Job certainly took this approach, and in 42:7 they are severely reprimanded for speaking this way: "My

wrath is kindled against you and against your two friends; for
you have not spoken of me what is right, as my servant Job
has" (NASB).

The fact of the matter is that in Scripture—most obviously in Job—it is often the person *favored* by God who suffers. To say that all suffering is punishment is to speak wrongly
of God!

Nor does it help simply to utter doctrinally correct things.
Job's friends all said many doctrinally correct things. But this
did not help Job deal with his own suffering. For example, in
Job 8 Bildad gives good sound doctrine. When Job answers
in Job 9, he acknowledges that Bildad's doctrine is correct:
"Indeed I know this is true . . ." (v. 2). But Job wants to know
how he can call God to account for the perceived discrep-
ancy between the theology and the reality he was experiencing. Similarly in Job 11 and 12. Job becomes almost sarcastic
in chapter 12: "Doubtless . . . wisdom will die with you" (v.
2). In other words, Job says, in effect, "You think I don't
know all this? Why do you think I've got cognitive dissonance? Sure these things are true, but I've got an existential
problem, not a doctrinal one." In fact, Job's existential problem presupposes the doctrine. If he did not believe in a just
and sovereign God, he would have no grounds for questioning God.

But what happens when God *does* answer Job? He does
not justify himself. He does not tell Job the reason for his
suffering, nor does he beg off from responsibility by saying,
"Hey, Job, I have to allow Satan some free will!" He only
points to his sovereign control of all in earth and heaven and
tells Job that Job has no wisdom. Yet ultimately God ends up
commending Job, precisely because Job acknowledges that
he does not understand what God is doing. Job's friends, who
were trying to justify God and come up with a logical explanation for Job's suffering, were sharply rebuked. The first les-

son of Job is that only God understands all he is doing, and it is best not to claim that we know why someone is suffering.

Second Lesson of Job: Honesty Is the Best Policy

At the end of Job, God commends him for speaking what is right about God (42:7). This is because Job remained completely honest. Job's cries to God are an example of the cries of an honest believer. Although Job's questions "darkened the counsel of God" (38:2), Job never stopped calling upon God. In the New Testament, James refers to Job as a great example of *patience and perseverance* (James 5:10–11).

Job does not look to us like a great example of either patience or piety; he complains bitterly chapter after chapter. He moves from simple complaint and confusion in the earlier chapters to outright accusation of God in the later. This ought to show us that the proper response to suffering is not "grinning and bearing it" or uttering pious platitudes. Job's perseverance consisted in his continuing to cling to God; he kept banging on God's door until he got a response. This is what a child does with an entirely trusted parent. When circumstances cause you, the child of God, to doubt your trust, you want reassurance. It is entirely legitimate to want reassurance, to desire some continuing evidence of God's love in the face of your suffering.

It is therefore foolish to try to manufacture some kind of artificial guilt trip to "justify" God or to get him to leave you alone. Unfortunately, this is often our response to suffering. But again, this is to assume that all suffering has a direct cause in our own actions. Job's friends were rebuked for trying to "justify" God, and Job was commended for not succumbing to their arguments and pretending to be guilty. When you are actually undergoing suffering, of course, it is perfectly understandable that you should try anything to "get God off

your case," because the need to make the suffering stop becomes overwhelming. People who have not experienced great
suffering have a difficult time realizing just how overwhelming this need can become. Nevertheless, to try to manipulate God into removing your suffering is to try to reduce him
to a capricious sort of god that characterized pagan religion, and
clearly God does not let himself be reduced to a pagan deity.

The second lesson of Job then, to remain openly honest, is
important if we are going to approach God at all. You cannot hide your true feelings from God, and God insists that
you not try. Unfortunately, some Christians think that such
honesty is inappropriate.

An insert in my church bulletin a few weeks ago, which
was dealing with prayer, raised the question whether it was
right to "tell God just how we feel." The insert answered
"No—we should always approach God with thankful hearts,"
as though it were somehow possible to conceal from God
just how we feel.

But the Bible does not say this. Not only Job, but all the
most godly characters in the Bible, including people writing
under inspiration, were very open about just how they felt.
Jeremiah shouts at God, "You deceived me" (Jer. 20:7). Naomi
exclaims, "Don't call me 'Pleasant,' call me 'Bitter' because
the Almighty has made my life very bitter" (Ruth 1:20). The
psalmist cries out, "Why have you forsaken me?" (Ps. 22:1).
Were these biblical writers sinning in such struggles with God?
Was Jesus praying improperly when he cried out, "Why have
you forsaken me?" Are the psalm writers sinning when they
only cry out and do not give thanks? Actually, Job's friends
did suggest it was wrong for Job to express to God his negative emotions (e.g. Job 15:25), but they were rebuked for their
dishonesty. Even if the biblical writers did sin by accusing
God, it would have been far worse to try to cover up their
struggles. Honesty is more important to God than niceness.

Indeed, to be the chosen of God means to be those who struggle with him, as the name "Israel" indicates (see Gen. 32:28). Jacob was called Israel because he struggled with God. The nation Israel too is the nation that struggles with God. To obtain God's blessing you must not give up or refuse to engage with him. Quiescent, passive refusal to engage, simply suggests you do not truly value the relationship—you just want to avoid conflict. Granted, our life with God is a struggle because we are still sinners, but it only compounds the sin if we try to avoid struggling honestly with God. There is no need for us to justify God, but we absolutely must encounter him.

Martin Luther was a great example of a man who was honest with God. Someone asked him once at a bad time whether he loved God. Luther's answer: "Love God? Sometimes I hate him." Luther surely was not denying God, and few people have been more passionately devoted to the Lord than Luther. But he was, like Job, extremely honest in his relationship—and look how God used him!

I think Psalm 88 is especially instructive here. In Psalm 88 the psalmist never receives an answer, never moves to thanksgiving, and never expresses trust or hope. The psalm ends with the dark words, "You have taken my companions and my loved ones from me, and darkness is my closest friend." But the psalmist never stopped *crying out to God*. Psalm 88 is a divinely inspired expression of faith. In the silence and the darkness, such passionate pleading and beating on the gate of heaven is precisely what faith must do. If you are in anguish, if you are still wondering where God is, if you feel precisely that your only friend is darkness, if you cannot at this moment say, "I trust you, God," Psalm 88 stands as a reminder that faith, though hidden, can still be present even in the pit of suffering and despair.

Psalm 116:10 is a very strange verse. It reads, "I believed;

therefore I said, 'I am greatly afflicted.' " It is so strange that some translations and commentaries have tried to make it say something more "reasonable." But this verse captures exactly what we are saying. Crying out to God is a *believing* response. It is *because* you believe that you bewail your condition before God. Of course, complaining *to* God is not the same as complaining *about* God to others. The Bible does not encourage us to grumble to others about God. But it does encourage us to be absolutely and totally honest in our struggle with God.

People who work with terminally ill patients tell me that most people, including believers, die poorly. They do not expire gracefully, calmly resting in faith and glowing with the hope of resurrection. Rather, they usually fall apart emotionally and spiritually, kicking and screaming at death. In many cases there is a dissolution of the mind prior to that of the body, which leaves the patient little facility for maintaining an attitude of faith in what is not seen. But Psalm 88 stands as a reminder that, simply because a person does not have the capacity to express his faith calmly and rationally does not mean that there is no faith. Even in the midst of his agonies and unceasing complaints against God, Job remained faithful, according to God's declaration at the end, because he never stopped struggling with God.

Job did not allow himself to be drawn into the kind of thinking that tries to "justify" God by shading the truth. He continued to maintain that his suffering was not caused by some sin of his, even though the resulting tension between what he knew and what he was experiencing remained unresolved. Job was not claiming that he was a morally perfect human being—he acknowledges in 14:16–17 that God will "cover over his sin"—but he did recognize that there was nothing in his life that was the direct cause of the suffering God had sent him.

Third Lesson of Job: It Ain't Over Till It's Over

At the end of the book of Job, two things happen: First, God answers Job out of the storm. Second, Job's health and happiness are restored, things are set right, and Job is commended for his integrity. God's answer to Job is not, however, what Job was asking for. Job wanted an explanation of his suffering. God gave him no explanation but simply reminded Job that he, God, is sovereign, not Job. But this reminder of God's sovereignty has an interesting element, in that it concludes with an entire chapter on "Leviathan." This chapter sounds simply like a description of a grand mythical beast, which only God, not Job, can tame. But "Leviathan" in the Old Testament is a symbol of the forces of evil and chaos that God overcomes. Earlier in Job (3:8) Leviathan is invoked as the representative of the curse against daytime and life. In Psalm 74:14 God is the one who "crushed the heads of Leviathan and gave him as food to the creatures of the desert." And in Isaiah 27 Leviathan is the enemy whom God will slay on judgment day.

> In that day the LORD with his hard and great and strong sword will punish Leviathan the fleeing serpent, Leviathan the twisting serpent, and he will slay the dragon that is in the sea. (v. 1 RSV)

In the New Testament this enemy of God is identified as Satan (see Rev. 12:9–10), the very accuser mentioned in Job 1 and 2. This is certainly consonant with God's description of Leviathan in Job 41, where he is "king over all that are proud" (v. 34). God calls attention to Leviathan's horrible strength in Job 41 to point out that God *does* have the Devil and the forces of chaos under control.[2] Here is the closure to Job 1 and 2. Yes, Satan is permitted to do a great deal of damage and is a mighty enemy, and he has caused a lot of suffering; but he cannot go beyond the limits set by God. And God is completely victorious in the end.

Psalm 34:19 reminds us, "Many are the afflictions of the righteous, but the LORD delivers him out of them all" (NASB). And Scripture consistently indicates that someday there will be a great weighing out when there *will* be complete justice and the righteous will have health and happiness forever restored. On that day everyone will be repaid according to what he has done (Isa. 3:10–14; Matt. 16:27; Rom. 2:6; 2 Cor. 5:10; Gal. 6:7–8; Rev. 2:23; 20:12).

Not only so, but the curse which results in suffering of every kind will finally be removed (Rev. 22:3), and as Revelation 21:4 tells us, God will wipe every tear from our eyes. Is there any image more tender than a mother's touch on the cheek, consoling her child by wiping away the tears?

The problem is, such expectations of future vindication may seem extremely remote and irrelevant when you are actually suffering. Although the Lord delivers us from them all, still the afflictions of the righteous are many. Knowing that the suffering will stop in the future may make the present suffering somewhat more bearable, but it does not answer the question of why the suffering had to happen in the first place. Further, it does not answer the question of why God does not immediately deliver us. Why does he wait so long to intervene?

Justice Now?

It might bother us a great deal when we see injustice that God does not deal with it *right away*. We want justice *now*. But let us think about that for a moment. *How* soon should God rectify wrong? Immediately? What if God did immediately pay back every evil deed, set to right every wrong, and reward every act of obedience? What would that mean for us?

First, if Romans 3:10 is right, it would mean instant death

and hell for everyone. Remember that *we sin too*. But, as D. A. Carson[3] pointed out, even if the penalty for sin were less than death and hell, immediate retribution would completely strip obedience of any meaning. Every act of obedience would simply be a response to an anticipated pleasure, and every refraining from disobedience would be purely out of desire to avoid pain. Smoldering resentment for this imposition would grow, and since God looks on the heart, further retribution would take place, and we would rapidly descend into an inescapable hell.

Second, if every sin had to be punished *immediately*, how could God the Son have borne the retribution vicariously at a time other than the sin itself? On the day of restoration of all righteousness, none who are covered with the blood of Christ will be complaining about unfairness. It is by wisdom and mercy that God refrains from delivering justice immediately (see 2 Peter 3:9). But he will deliver justice eventually. Longfellow's words are worth remembering:

> The mills of God grind slowly,
>   yet they grind exceeding small.
> Though with patience He stands waiting,
>   with exactness grinds He all.

Yet we do have hope, not only for justice but also for our deliverance in God's good time. In a way, faith itself is this hope. To hope is constantly to maintain one's focus on the future that we do not yet have. As Hebrews says, faith is being "certain of what we do not [yet] see" (11:1). Job at least at one point recognized this even as he was undergoing his suffering, and even though he could not understand why God would let him suffer. He was therefore able to express his hope for a deliverer, even when he was beginning to wonder if God was his enemy.

The Redeemer Shall Arise

In Job 13:15 Job makes a remarkable statement: "Though he slay me, yet will I hope in him." How can Job put his hope in God if God is slaying him? Why trust a God who is doing you hurt? What is the point in having hoped in God if you are dead? The reason Job can say this is seen in Job 19:25–26, where he utters that wonderful testimony to his hope for the future:

> I know that my Redeemer lives,
>   and that in the end he will stand upon the earth.
> And after my skin has been destroyed,
>   yet in my flesh I will see God;
> I myself will see him
>   with my own eyes—I, and not another
> How my heart yearns within me!

This is actually an amazing passage, because Job in the context of chapter 19 describes God as his enemy (vv. 10–12):

> He [God] tears me down on every side till I am
>   gone;
>   he uproots my hope like a tree.
> His anger burns against me;
>   he counts me among his enemies.
> His troops advance in force;
>   they build a siege ramp against me
>   and encamp around my tent.

And yet he hopes for vindication. He expects a go'el, a kinsman redeemer, at the end to vindicate him before God. It is wise to be cautious about just how much Job really understood, and it is notoriously difficult to determine exactly what this passage means, but Job at least seems to know that there is an Advocate-Mediator who will interpose himself before God on Job's behalf. Earlier, in 9:33–34, Job cried out,

> If only there were someone to arbitrate between us,
>   to lay his hand upon us both,
> someone to remove God's rod from me,
>   so that his terror would frighten me no more.

Now in chapter 19 he declares his faith that there is such a Mediator. Usually such an advocate or *go'el* is a close relative. The book of Ruth tells the story of how Naomi's kinsman Boaz acted as *go'el* for Naomi and Ruth. At some cost to himself, Boaz intervenes to rescue his cousins from destitution and ensures their inheritance. Does Job in the midst of his suffering have some glimpse of Jesus, the older-brother/Redeemer, who will ultimately stand upon the earth and serve as Advocate for Job before God? Whether he does or not, it is clear he has confidence that, even if it takes place after his death, some day he will be vindicated and will somehow *witness* his vindication (see also Job 23:10). It may even be that, since the *go'el* of the downtrodden and afflicted is God himself (Prov. 23:11; Jer. 50:34; Ps. 119:154), Job knows that God himself will somehow be the Advocate who will plead Job's cause before himself, even as we now know that God the Son ever lives to intercede for us before God the Father (Heb. 7:25).

Nevertheless, this vindication, the rectifying, was only in the future for Job when he uttered this great confession. At the moment of suffering, the affliction is really hard for anyone to take, even someone like "patient" Job. The New International Version translation of the last line of verse 27, "my heart yearns within me," does not quite convey the emotional power of the original, which means something like "my emotions are completely wiped out over this." Patiently awaiting God's solution is not something Job could do coolly. And we should not be surprised when we cannot remain cool either.

Conclusion

Job's lessons should be heard both by the sufferer and by the friends of sufferers. We cannot assume that the one who suffers "must not be in the center of God's will" or has somehow offended God. Certainly we cannot lay the burden on sufferers that "if they just had enough faith God would heal or deliver them." This is insidious and is clearly condemned by God at the end of Job. Neither can we suppose that we can always figure out what God is up to when we endure suffering. Rather, both sufferers and the friends of sufferers need patience, not as a stoical endurance, but as an unrelenting clinging to God, even when he appears to be an enemy, in confidence that our Redeemer has indeed stood on the earth and interceded for us, and we need to await the day when God will put things right.

But even though we know that some day God will set everything right, and even though we can see some of the reasons why he does not repay evil immediately, there is still mystery as to why he allows evil to begin with. Why did he simply not allow any evil, including suffering, to enter his universe?

Jesus says in the Beatitudes, "Blessed are they who mourn, for they shall be comforted." This certainly expects a future setting-to-rights, but why should those who mourn be considered blessed? Would it not be better to have no grief at all than to have it and then be comforted?

The only answer to this mystery is to point to another mystery. Somehow the suffering of Christians links them to

Jesus Christ in a special way. Job 19:25 indicates that Job had some inkling of a Mediator who would prove to be the solution to the problem of suffering. We now have the full revelation of our union with Christ. This brings us to our next chapter, which asks specifically why those who believe in Christ must suffer.

For Further Consideration

1. What are the chief lessons of the book of Job? How do these lessons differ from what the unbelieving world says?
2. Have you ever cried out to God the way Job did? Have you ever been in such a pit of despair that you felt like the author of Psalm 88? How were things resolved for you?
3. Do you think Job was sinning when he complained to God about what was happening to him? What is the difference between complaining *to* God and complaining *about* him? How does this distinction apply in our relationship to other people?
4. Have you ever tried to "comfort" someone in the manner of Job's friends? Where did the friends go wrong? How can we *truly* comfort those who are suffering?
5. Why did God use such strange imagery in describing his sovereignty in Job 38–40? What has that speech to do with the problem of human suffering?
6. If someone's suffering is in the mind, such as depression or anxiety or even something more severe like schizophrenia, do you think this is always due to sin on the sufferer's part? Why or why not?

NOTES

1. Perhaps the closest to an all-encompassing explanation for suffering that safeguards the sovereignty of God is the "grand demonstra-

tion" view, that God allows evil (including suffering) the more to demonstrate his own glory and mercy to his sentient creatures, both men and angels (cf. Jay Adams, *The Grand Demonstration: A Biblical Study of the So-Called Problem of Evil* [Santa Barbara: EastGate, 1991]). He allows his children to suffer in order to demonstrate his power in changing the character of formerly fallen humans. But this explanation still leaves mystery, because it is very unclear to us why angels or people would applaud God for being so unprotective of those who have most fully entrusted themselves to him.

2. Job cannot "put a hook in Leviathan's snout," but the implication is that God can. The same language is used in Isaiah 37:29 to refer to the fact that God has complete control over Sennacherib, to whom God says, "I will put My hook in your nose, and My bridle in your lips, and I will turn you back by the way by which you came" (NASB).

3. D. A. Carson, *How Long O Lord* (Grand Rapids: Baker, 1990), 181.

Chapter 5

Why Do Christians Suffer? (1)
Suffering with Christ

I WONDER IF I am rejecting Job's advice just by asking the question, "Why do Christians suffer?" If we cannot definitively answer the general question "Why is there unjust suffering?" then how can we ask why *we* suffer? Yet Deuteronomy 29:29 tells us that, although the secret things belong to God, the revealed things belong to us and to our children. The Bible does tell us *some* of the reasons why God allows his children to suffer, although it does not allow us to give an answer for every particular instance.

The book of 1 Peter, perhaps more than any other book in the Bible, tries to answer the question of why Christians suffer. It does this by talking a lot about Christ's suffering. First Peter is full of wonderful statements about the meaning of Christ's suffering and death. But the primary purpose for these statements is to connect Christ's suffering to the questions of how to live the Christian life—in particular, why believers are suffering and how they ought to respond to it.

To a large degree the whole Christian life is a response to

suffering. After all, when things are going well, we do not need spiritual resources and exhortations to persevere. How we handle life is a question of how we handle suffering. First Peter is helpful precisely because it applies the great truths of the gospel to our need as sufferers.

Scripture in general and 1 Peter in particular identify two basic reasons for the suffering of God's children: (1) identification with Christ and (2) discipline, both in a negative sense of punishment and in the positive sense of purifying and training. By far the most important of these is the identification with Christ that suffering entails; the disciplinary function of suffering depends on that. Our suffering as believers connects us to Christ. This connection to Christ by means of suffering makes our suffering meaningful—it transforms our suffering into something redemptive rather than destructive. This is so not because our suffering itself is redemptive, but because it connects us to Christ's suffering. And *Christ's* suffering certainly means something.

Christ's Suffering

"I feel your pain," says the politician, hoping people will believe his expressions of sympathy. Usually, however, we do not believe people who say that unless we know they have really experienced something similar or are suffering from the same cause.

Christians believe that God can sympathize because he experienced our weakness as well as our pain (Heb. 2:18; 4:15). This chapter will dwell on something more than just God's sympathy, however. Isaiah 53 says that Christ not only can sympathize, but that he has *carried* our griefs and sorrows. This means more than just that he took the punishment that should have been ours. The context in Isaiah is of the suffering of God's people in exile. The servant of the

Lord has taken on himself those very sufferings of his people. Not only does he know what it is like—he actually experiences our sufferings with us. The closest thing in human experience is perhaps when a parent sees her or his child suffering.

God's suffering with his people is a dominant theme in 1 Peter, which assumes the central significance of Isaiah 53, especially the idea of *vicarious* suffering, suffering in our place. Peter then applies it to our own experience of suffering, which is, after all, little bits of death. Christ suffered for us; we suffer in Christ.

> For Christ also suffered for sins once for all, the righteous for the unrighteous, in order to bring you to God. (1 Peter 3:18 NRSV)

> Christ suffered for you, leaving you an example, that you should follow in his steps. (2:21)

> He himself bore our sins in his body on the tree, so that we might die to sins and live for righteousness; by his wounds you have been healed. (2:24)

Here is the marvelous, distinctly Christian answer to suffering. First, we must see that the suffering of Christ had a very clear purpose and meaning. Second, our suffering identifies us with the God who suffered.

If Jesus' suffering did not have meaning and purpose, then it was simply pitiable. What purpose could it have had unless it actually accomplished something? Likewise, our suffering, if it has no purpose, is simply pitiful, not something to be understood—certainly not something to *rejoice* in (1 Peter 4:13; cf. Col. 1:24). But Peter, like the rest of the New Testament writers, insists that Christ's suffering has a very clear purpose, both in dealing with sin and in linking himself to us.

This is not a book about the atonement, but we must be reminded that if Jesus' death did not actually accomplish anything, then his suffering does not mean anything, and neither does ours. If his death was *only* to show us how much he loved us, then in fact it does not show us how much he loved us, but only shows that he was foolish. If a friend jumped out of a boat and gave his life in order to save a drowning person, we would see it as an act of love, but if he jumped out and died just to "show" the people on shore how much he loved them or to show "how to die nobly," we would say he was crazy. But in fact, it is precisely because Christ's death *actually* rescues us and actually destroys death itself by removing the curse, that Peter and the other New Testament writers can say that the suffering of Christians in Christ has meaning.

The God Who Knows Suffering

Perhaps the main reason that Christians insist that God can be trusted in the midst of suffering is that we remember that God himself has firsthand experience of suffering. A Greek proverb reads, "A fool learns from what he suffers." And sin has made us stupid, so that we must suffer in order to learn. Hebrews tells us, amazingly, that *Jesus* learned from what he suffered (Heb. 5:8), not because he was a foolish sinner, but because he identified himself with foolish sinners (see Isa. 53:12, "he was numbered with the transgressors"). The cross reminds us that God himself knows what it is like to suffer, and he has already carried the bulk of the suffering that results from sin—and has triumphed. As Jesus Christ endured and thus overcame suffering, so are we enabled to endure.

Why is it that the narrative of Christ's suffering, the so-called "Passion Narrative," was so immensely popular through most of the church's history prior to this century? Probably because people of most centuries have experienced a great deal of suffering in their lives—and knowing a God who has suffered is immensely comforting. God knows what it is like to suffer, not just because he sees it in far greater clarity than we, but because he has personally suffered in the most severe way possible, the disruption of his own family (the Trinity) by the immensity of his own wrath against sin.

Now we must be careful here, when we speak of God as the suffering God. Some people think that the suffering of Christ portrays God as the vulnerable, victimized, and pathetic sympathizer who cannot do anything and so suffers alongside us, feeling our frustrations just as we do when we helplessly see our children suffer. According to this view, God showed his love for us by sending his Son so that he could suffer and die while God stood helplessly by and watched. But while it is good to have a friend who knows what it is like to stand by helplessly, this is not the kind of God we need, and it is not the kind of God we have in the Bible. The Bible portrays God as *victorious over* suffering and death. The reason for sending his Son was not just to experience suffering but to conquer and destroy sin and suffering. The story did not end with the crucifixion. The death of Christ was the death of death.

But the reminder that God knows suffering in Jesus does guard us against overdoing the "impassibility" of God, which theologians sometimes talk about, as though God, because he is unchangeable, can never be moved with compassion or experience emotion. The Bible speaks again and again of his being moved with compassion, of taking pity, of being angry, of taking delight. True, God does not have "emotions" in the same way we do (with neurochemical processes, subject to changes over time), but neither does God "think" the same way we do (with a brain, in chronological sequence), and rarely does any Christian suggest that God has no thoughts! Our true thoughts are patterned after God's thoughts, and our emotions are patterned after something in God as well.

Thus we can speak of the suffering God, because God has experienced the agony of loss by death, the separation from a beloved, and the hatred of men. But he experienced these things not helplessly, but conqueringly. We have a Father who can and will "fix it."

According to 1 Peter 2:21, suffering is God's sovereign intention for his people, because they must follow in Christ's footsteps. Suffering benefits believers as the covenantal experience of divine judgment in Christ, which sanctifies them and indicts the world. Suffering somehow links believers to Christ in a way no other earthly experience can do.

Suffering Ties the Believer to Christ

Suffering produces solidarity between people. In spite of the difficulties and hardships of the Great Depression, many people who lived through it remember it as a time when people came to each other's assistance, and a sense of community was very strong. Even now, when a neighborhood is hit by natural disaster or war, the neighbors who barely knew one another by sight will draw together and become a real community.

An even better example is the story of Ewald and Willi, who were children in Germany during World War II. Before the war they, like many siblings, fought with and despised each other. After the war, living on their own without parents, they survived by begging and stealing from the Americans, and became the closest of brothers. It was a horrible time for them, but to this day they are extremely close. Yet these examples are but a pale shadow of the degree to which Christ's suffering links him with us, God's covenant people.

The sense of covenant identity is so powerful in the Bible that Christ's suffering and death has actually *become* the suffering and death of his people. We have been crucified with Christ, says Paul (Gal. 2:20). The reverse is also true: the suffering and death of his people is also in some way Christ's suffering and death. So 1 Peter tells us that, as Jesus was put to death in flesh but made alive by (the) Spirit (3:18), so men were judged in the flesh but live to God by (the) Spirit (4:6). Our point here is that *Christian suffering is Christological:* "You participate in the sufferings of Christ" (4:13). Thus our suffering, while never desirable in itself, is nevertheless to be treasured. James 1 says, "Count it all joy," and Matthew 5 says, "Rejoice when men persecute you for my sake."

Paul speaks of our sufferings as "having fellowship" with the sufferings of Christ. In fact Paul connects this to his doctrine of the righteousness of God that comes through faith. In Philippians 3 he says, "Everything that might be said to be to my credit I count as trash, in order that I might gain Christ and be found in him, not having my own righteousness by law but righteousness through faith in Christ, the righteousness that is from God on the basis of faith, in order that I might know him and the power of his resurrection *and the fellowship of his sufferings, being conformed to his death*" (vv. 8–10 NKJV). Christians share in Christ's suffering, and this suffering with Christ is a privilege that confirms one's righteousness through him.

This is also why Paul can make the amazing claim that his sufferings "fill up" what is lacking in the sufferings of Christ (Col. 1:24). Paul makes it abundantly clear throughout his writings that the sufferings of Christ and Christ alone have accomplished redemption entirely, and we add nothing to it. But in some way, the suffering of Paul is so closely linked to

his Lord's suffering that it has a part in that redemptive activity. Suffering in Christ is a wonderful privilege. Paul's suffering, and I believe the righteous suffering of every believer,
has meaning, because it is tied up with Christ's meaningful
suffering.

Why are the sacraments that symbolize our union with
Christ so gruesome? Why the broken body and the blood?
Because they point to his suffering! When we take communion, we identify with Christ in his suffering and death. We
declare ourselves as taking on the suffering of Christ. Communion reminds us that Christ's suffering has meaning and
our sharing in that suffering has meaning.

It is unfortunate that we do not stress communion more in
our churches, because the sacrament is a tangible, physical
reminder that very powerfully symbolizes our connectedness
to the suffering and death of Jesus. People who are suffering
usually do not get a great deal of encouragement from doctrine unless that doctrine is made personal somehow. Job
certainly got little from the "sound doctrine" that his friends
recited to him *ad nauseam*. He did obtain some encouragement from his conviction that his kinsman redeemer would
eventually arise, because this was not just a propositional
truth, but a real person. Communion reinforces for us our
personal connectedness with Jesus, and it is this, not just the
bare propositional truths about Jesus, that are the Christian
sufferer's lifeline. This is not to minimize the importance of
propositional truth. But it will not be important to us until it
is personal. And when we suffer, Christ's suffering becomes
much more personal.

Such identification with Jesus' suffering is also the source
of hope. Christ learned humanhood from his suffering
(Heb. 5:8). We learn Christhood from our suffering. Therefore, *our* story does not end with suffering and death either. As Paul says:

If we have been united with him like this in his death,
we will certainly also be united with him in his resurrection. (Rom. 6:5)

But thanks be to God! He gives us the victory through
our Lord Jesus Christ. (1 Cor. 15:57)

If we share in Christ's death, we will also share in his resurrection. As Paul says over and over again, we who have
died with Christ will also be raised with him, and indeed we
are already in some sense raised with him in anticipation of
that event (Rom. 6:4; 8:11; 1 Cor. 15:12–20; Eph. 2:6; Col.
3:1). Our being already raised with him means we are already being made like him.

Living Stones and the Living Stone

As Christ has identified with us by his suffering, so we are
identified with Jesus by our suffering, and we begin to take
on his character. Peter represents this in a symbolic way in
his comparison of believers as stones to Christ the living stone
of Isaiah 8:14; Isaiah 28:16; and Psalm 118:22.

As you come to him, the living Stone—rejected by
men but chosen by God and precious to him—you
also, like living stones, are being built into a spiritual
house to be a holy priesthood, offering spiritual sac-
rifices acceptable to God through Jesus Christ. For in
Scripture it says:

"See, I lay a stone in Zion,
   a chosen and precious cornerstone,
and the one who trusts in him
   will never be put to shame."

Now to you who believe, this stone is precious. But to those who do not believe,

> "The stone the builders rejected
> has become the capstone,"

and,

> "A stone that causes men to stumble
> and a rock that makes them fall."

They stumble because they disobey the message—which is also what they were destined for.

But you are a chosen people, a royal priesthood, a holy nation, a people belonging to God, that you may declare the praises of him who called you out of darkness into his wonderful light. (1 Peter 2:4–9)

The foundation stone, "capstone" (v. 7), or "cornerstone" (v. 6) is clearly Jesus. As Peter points out, the Old Testament prophesied that people would reject this one on whom the people of God (God's house) would be built. How could a sufferer be the foundation stone? The idea of a suffering Messiah was unacceptable to most Jews. Yet it was precisely this rejected suffering Messiah whom God chose as the "foundation stone." Peter goes on to point out that, just as people rejected the chief stone, so they will reject all other "stones" who are connected to him.

Is it not strange how people turn away from others who are suffering, so that the sufferer suffers twice—first the pain and loss itself and then the loss of friends? Jesus himself in the moment of his greatest affliction was abandoned by most of his friends. Sometimes, that happens to us. As the chief stone suffered, all the stones can expect to suffer. Yet the chief stone and the other stones as well, by virtue of their connection to him, are precious to God (vv. 4, 9), in spite of, or perhaps even because of, their suffering and rejection.

There is a great mystery here. Somehow suffering connects Christ to us and us to Christ, and this is what enables us both to know that he shares in our experience of suffering and to share in his sufferings and glory. Suffering is what made Jesus the foundation stone of his people. Suffering is also what makes us stones that are built on that foundation.

God's Judgment and God's People

Peter gets to the heart of this mystery when he says that "it is the season when judgment begins with the household of God" (4:17 my translation). This seems very strange, for Peter has claimed that those who suffer "for doing what is right" are *blessed*. How can suffering for doing right be termed a beginning of judgment from God?

Suffering is a judgment because it causes a discernment, a sorting out of good from bad; it is like a trial by ordeal (cf. 3:20–21 where the flood, God's judgment, was the means of Noah's deliverance from wickedness). Suffering enables a Christian to see his own evil clearly and equips him to purge it. It also enables him to see his connection to Christ more clearly.

These aspects of suffering (sharing in Jesus' suffering and divine judgment) are linked. First Peter appears to use "suffering" in much the same way that Paul uses "dying" as a term for covenantal identification. Thus for example in 1 Peter 2:21 (and probably also 3:18, although manuscripts vary), we have "Christ *suffered* for you," just as Paul would say "Christ *died* for you." Just as baptism in Romans is presented as a *sacramental* identification with Christ, suffering is presented in 1 Peter as an *experiential* identification with

Christ. So in 1 Peter 4:1, "He who has *suffered* . . . has ceased from sin" is analogous to Paul's comment in Romans 6:2–4, which says in effect that "he who has been *baptized* has died to sin."

The point is that the suffering and dying of Christ were the means God used to connect Christ to his people. Suffering is therefore also the means God uses to apply that connection experientially to us. Those who share in Christ's suffering share also in his judgment—both his condemnation of sin in his death and his righteous vindication afterward. We see here most manifestly the principle of 1 Peter 1:11–12 that the prophecies of the sufferings of Christ and the glories following are also "for you."

All this has a very practical outworking in our lives. Identifying with Christ in his suffering is the source of the purifying and discipling aspect of suffering we will discuss later. Look for a moment at the passage we just referred to, 1 Peter 4:1.

> Therefore, since Christ suffered in his body, arm yourselves also with the same attitude, because he who has suffered in his body is done with sin.

This sounds like suffering causes a person to become sinless, but certainly we know sufferers who are still great sinners. The point is that if we have suffered in Christ, then we no longer are in sin's domain. For Paul, the believer has died in Christ, but must also die daily. Again note that 1 Peter uses "suffer" in much the same way that Paul uses "die." Compare these statements with Romans 6:5–10:

> If we have been united with him like this in his death, we will certainly also be united with him in his resurrection. For we know that our old self was crucified with him so that the body of sin might be

done away with, that we should no longer be slaves to sin—because anyone who has died has been freed from sin.

Now if we died with Christ, we believe that we will also live with him. For we know that since Christ was raised from the dead, he cannot die again; death no longer has mastery over him. The death he died, he died to sin once for all; but the life he lives, he lives to God.

Paul says that Christ has died for us, and so we have died with Christ. For Peter, the believer has suffered in Christ, but must also suffer now. The present experience of suffering is simply an outworking of the already accomplished identification with Christ in suffering. Suffering is not only past (4:1) but also must be ongoing (4:13—note the present tense: "rejoice that you [presently] participate in the sufferings of Christ . . ."). Paul seems to be referring to suffering in a similar way in 2 Corinthians 4:11: "For we who are alive are always being given over to death for Jesus' sake, so that his life may be revealed in our mortal body." First Peter 4:2–3 goes on to say that this should be motivation for no longer sinning:

> As a result, he does not live the rest of his earthly life for evil human desires, but rather for the will of God. For you have spent enough time in the past doing what pagans choose to do—living in debauchery, lust, drunkenness, orgies, carousing and detestable idolatry.

Compare this with what Paul says in Romans 6:1–4:

> What shall we say, then? Shall we go on sinning so that grace may increase? By no means! We died to

sin; how can we live in it any longer? Or don't you
know that all of us who were baptized into Christ
Jesus were baptized into his death? We were therefore buried with him through baptism into death in
order that, just as Christ was raised from the dead
through the glory of the Father, we too may live a
new life.

We earlier noted how Christ carried our sins by his suffering, so that we might die to sins and live for righteousness (1
Peter 2:24). It is interesting that Peter here in 2:24 does not
use any of the usual words for "die." He uses rather a word
that more generally means to depart or to cease having any
part in. Christ's identification with our suffering means that
our suffering *in him* is a departure from sins. Thus the idea of
suffering as *discipline* or *purification* (see chapter 8 below) takes
on a new dimension. By linking us to Christ's suffering, our
own suffering makes us like Christ and thus free from the
dominion of sin. Paul found that he must die daily (1 Cor.
15:31); Peter reminds us that we must suffer daily. Our daily
dying/suffering progressively divorces us from sin, so that we
no longer live for our own pleasure but for God's pleasure.

Thus when Peter says in 1 Peter 4:17 that judgment is beginning with the house of God, he is placing the suffering of
Christians in its redemptive context. Even as the judgment
fell on Christ, so we in Christ experience something of the
judgment of God, not for our own sin, but as part of the great
work of redemption in and through Christ. We are not condemned at the end of history, because we have already faced
death in Christ. And this pre-experiencing of judgment gives
us power over our spiritual enemies even now. Remember
that 4:1 tells us to arm ourselves with this thought, that the
one who has suffered has ceased from sin. Suffering, far from
being meaningless, prepares us for combat with the forces of

evil—it enables us to do good. Therefore, as Peter says, we have every reason for committing ourselves to the faithful Creator in doing good.

For Further Consideration

1. Is God a victim of suffering? If he is, how can we say he is in control? If he is not, how can he really sympathize with us when we don't have any choice but to suffer?
2. How does the suffering of Jesus make our suffering meaningful?
3. If you have suffered, did you think of it as suffering with Christ? Why or why not?
4. If God is infinite, eternal, and unchangeable, how can he be "moved" by anything that happens to us?
5. What does God's judgment have to do with suffering in Christ?
6. Have you ever experienced being drawn closer to someone because of suffering together? Do you find that suffering draws you closer to God or drives you further from him? Why would it do one, rather than the other?
7. Has your experience of suffering helped you to overcome sin or prepared you to resist it?

CHAPTER 6

Why Do Christians Suffer? (2)
Suffering as Testimony

FIRST PETER 4 points out that the fruit of suffering, that we live to please God, does not go unnoticed by unbelievers. They do not understand it, and sometimes they react to the life they see in believers by persecuting them. This is especially true when a new believer stops participating in the sins of his or her former partners in sin (4:3–4). I remember in my college days how, when someone became a Christian, usually the first and most continuing hardship that person faced as a new Christian was dealing with roommates and friends who became angry and sarcastic.

Peter several times indicates that a major reason why Christians suffer, and the reason they ought to suffer, is simply because they are Christians. Especially note 1 Peter 4:15–16:

> If you suffer, it should not be as a murderer or thief or any other kind of criminal, or even as a meddler. However, if you suffer as a Christian, do not be ashamed, but praise God that you bear that name.

He is simply echoing the teaching of Jesus (John 15:20–21):

> "No servant is greater than his master." If they persecuted me, they will persecute you also. . . . They will treat you this way because of my name, for they do not know the One who sent me.

Suffering in Christ is a wonderful testimony. The great "mandate for apologetics" in 1 Peter 3:15—to be always ready with a defense for the hope that is within you—is found in the context of a passage about suffering, partly because suffering is a problem and partly because the Christian's ability to answer for that hope in the face of suffering is one of the church's most effective tools of witness. Paul told the Philippian Christians that he was suffering "for the defense of the gospel" (Phil. 1:16). Further, Paul's suffering was not only a testimony to such people as the Praetorian Guard (Caesar's household), but it became an encouragement to other Christians to share the gospel (Phil. 1:14). Since suffering in Christ is so effective in witness and such a testimony to the faithfulness of God, Paul regards it as a privilege to suffer, and he tells the Philippians that they also have this privilege (Phil. 1:29). As Tertullian observed, the blood of martyrs is the seed of the church.

What Suffering Counts?

The commendation of suffering, not only in 1 Peter but also elsewhere in the New Testament, is focused on suffering for the sake of Christ. "If you suffer as a Christian . . . praise God that you bear that name" (1 Peter 4:16). Participating in the sufferings of Christ (4:13) means, above all, being afflicted precisely because one is a Christian. Does this mean that only persecution of Christians specifically *because* they are Christians links us to Christ's suffering?

Peter actually gives warrant for saying that *all* suffering that we endure for Christ's sake identifies us with Christ. In 1 Peter 2, slaves who suffered under "harsh masters" were not necessarily suffering specifically because they identified them-selves as Christians. Slaves frequently suffered just because their masters were arbitrary and unjust. But they did never-theless suffer like Christ (vv. 20–21), because they suffered not for doing evil but for doing good. The fact that they clung to Christ while they endured suffering is what made their suffering meaningful. Peter says (2:19), "It is commendable if a man bears up under the pain of unjust suffering because he is conscious of God." What makes an occasion of suffer-ing a suffering "for the sake of Christ"? Is it the motivation of the person or agent causing the affliction? No, it is the atti-tude or conscience of the person who is suffering. Thus any affliction can be suffering for Christ, when we endure it for Christ's sake.

Does this mean that suffering because of illness or acci-dent can be suffering "for Christ's sake"? Yes, indeed. Re-member that Job suffered righteously and was commended for it. His suffering was brought about not by people who afflicted him for his faith but by Satan. According to Jesus, oppressive illness is an affliction by Satan (Luke 13:16). Thus Jesus' healing ministry was an aspect of his defeat of Satan (see Acts 10:38: "Jesus . . . went around doing good and heal-ing all who were under the power of the devil, because God was with him"). And certainly Satan afflicts us with diseases, bondage, and oppression because of our faith in God. It brings glory to God therefore when we endure suffering for Christ's sake, because it is a victory over Satan. This victory over Satan is probably the primary reason why Peter includes the bit about "preaching to the spirits in prison" in 1 Peter 3.

Christ Preached to the Spirits in Prison

First Peter 3:18–22 is a very strange passage that many people simply pass over. It has been understood in a number of ways, but there are really only two options that are at all likely.[1]

1. Augustine believed that Peter was referring to Christ's proclaiming the gospel to the people prior to the Flood through the lips of Noah, who was warning the people of the coming wrath. No doubt Noah would have experienced a great deal of ridicule and verbal abuse from such preaching, even as the Christians in 1 Peter's purview experienced slander. Even if Noah were not "preaching" in the usual sense of the word (Genesis says nothing about Noah trying to warn his neighbors), the very fact that he was preparing against the coming deluge was a testimony to his belief in God's judgment. If this is the correct interpretation, it reminds us that even though we suffer now in testimony, our vindication is sure.

2. The other option is that Peter was drawing on the Jewish legend of the godly Enoch announcing judgment against the evil angels. Although there is nothing to this effect in Genesis, there was a popular book now known as *I Enoch* that told this story in detail. On this view Peter, by drawing on this legend, was indicating that Christ proclaimed victory over such evil angels by his death and resurrection. Jesus would then have been a "greater Enoch" who suffered but was vindicated. Certainly in 3:22 we see Jesus as victorious over the "angels, authorities and powers," the evil spirits that controlled the old age. And there are many linguistic parallels between this passage and *I Enoch* that encourage many scholars to adopt this view.

If this is what Peter was doing, this too would encourage Christians in their suffering. The ancient world saw life, including evil, in much more personal terms than we do today. We have sanitized and depersonalized evil. But for people

who knew that Satan and his cohorts were behind the persecution and oppression of Christians (as we see, for example,
in Revelation), this passage would remind them that the evil
spirits, who now seemed to have so much power and who
perpetrate all kinds of suffering upon God's people, are already defeated by the death and resurrection of Jesus. Further, on this interpretation, the suffering of Christ itself
becomes a witness, albeit a negative one to the demons, that
God is faithful in suffering.

But whether this passage is understood as Christ's proclamation of victory over the evil angels or Christ's preaching
salvation through the lips of Noah, the point is that Christ's
suffering is itself a proclamation—a testimony of God's
faithfulness. Jesus suffered, but he was also raised, and now is
seated at God's right hand, victorious over every enemy. The
path to exaltation lies through the valley of suffering. And
this is why the Scriptures repeatedly indicate that it is the
calling of Christians to suffer in a certain way. So 2 Timothy
3:12 for example: "Everyone who wants to live a godly life in
Christ Jesus *will be* persecuted." It is very clear that suffering,
including suffering at the hands of other people, and certainly at the hands of Satan, is inescapable for the Christian.

It is not surprising therefore that we are told "always to be
ready." It is difficult to be ready all the time. Peter, like Paul,
frequently uses military terminology to describe the Christian life (for example, 1:13; 4:1). People who have been in
combat know that such readiness is difficult but essential.
Days, weeks, months of inaction will go by, and then two
days of very intense action. As 1 Peter 4:12 reminds us, we
are not to be surprised by suffering, but be ready for it—so
that our suffering can be a witness.

This does not have to be physical affliction—in fact in 1
Peter all the specific indications of suffering except for abused
slaves appear to be verbal: "when men revile you, speak slan-

derously against you," etc. (see 2:12; 3:16; 4:4, 14). Likewise
the famous saying of Jesus in Matthew 5—"Blessed are you
when men revile you, and persecute you, and say all kinds of
evil against you" (v. 11 NASB)—is concerned largely with
verbal abuse. Usually physical persecution is preceded by a
build-up of verbal abuse. It is an amazing testimony to the
power of God that in spite of such slandering, God uses such
suffering to reach non-Christians.

And They'll Know We Are Christians by Our Suffering

Suffering somehow *wins* people. I think this is because suffering is a great "weigher-out" of what a person's true character is. Earlier we discussed the fact that suffering can be a
testing. You cannot do much pretending when you are suffering. When a non-Christian sees how a Christian struggles
with God, and yet cannot cease to relate to God (even if
only in anger or questioning), it makes his or her own emptiness acute. The non-Christian has no focus, no reason why
it is appropriate to ask "Why?" Although our suffering in
Christ is not vicariously redemptive, it is redemptive in the
sense that *our suffering displays Christ's suffering* and therefore
can be used by God as a means of touching non-Christians.

Peter notes this in 1 Peter 5:1. He declares that he is a
witness to the sufferings of Christ. This verse is the opening
to Peter's exhortation to the church leaders (5:1–4), and it is
often missed that it comes right after his exhortation to those
who are suffering according to the will of God to entrust themselves to the faithful Creator in doing good (4:19). Thus when
Peter declares that he is a witness of the sufferings of Christ
and a partaker in the glory soon to be revealed, he is con-
necting again the sufferings of the people with Christ's sufferings. I do not think Peter is here referring to his having
seen the crucifixion—the account in the Gospels suggests

Peter had run away and John was the only one of the Twelve who actually saw the crucifixion. Rather, Peter is referring to the fact that he *bears testimony* to Christ's suffering. Possibly he may even be hinting that he himself has experienced suffering and therefore is also a partaker in the glory (cf. Rom. 8:17). In any case, the injunction that sufferers should entrust themselves to God (1 Peter 4:19) must be related to the testimony to Christ's suffering in 5:1, because "entrusting himself to God" is what Jesus did. Such trust activity produces a dividend, because as others see that echo of Jesus, the Holy Spirit may move some of them to place their own trust in the faithful Creator.

We should thank God that insurance companies generally only cover semiprivate rooms—because non-Christians get to observe how Christians suffer. And Christians, knowing that their suffering is being observed, are more aware of their calling to suffer in a certain way. I think a case could be made that this is one of the most effective ways we have of bearing testimony.

Thus, in some sense our suffering for the sake of Christ is often instrumental not just for our own growth, but for the spiritual birth and growing of others. Paul in 2 Corinthians 4:10–12 points out that his suffering results in blessing to the Corinthians.

> We always carry around in our body the death of Jesus, so that the life of Jesus may also be revealed in our body. For we who are alive are always being given over to death for Jesus' sake, so that his life may be revealed in our mortal body. So then, death is at work in us, but life is at work in you.

Note that Paul says death is *at work*. God is using Paul's "death" (here a reference to the afflictions that mark Paul's union with Christ) in order to produce life in the Corinthians. The obvious analogy here is to the pangs of childbearing. The agony of the mother produces life for the child. A mother giving birth does not enjoy the pain, but she is willing to endure it for the sake of her baby. Paul's affliction benefited the Corinthians. Stephen's suffering benefited Paul. The origin of this pattern is in Jesus' suffering for all his children. Through Jesus, death produces life.

This is what Paul means when he says in Colossians 1:24,

> Now I rejoice in what was suffered for you, and I fill up in my flesh what is still lacking in regard to Christ's afflictions, for the sake of his body, which is the church.

Christ's suffering bore fruit in the people for whom he died; Paul says that his own suffering also, as a further working out of Christ's suffering, is bearing fruit in the lives of Christ's people. Thus the principle of one person's suffering bearing fruit in another person's life continues. Are we willing to share in Christ's sufferings to the extent that our suffering is useful, not to ourselves, but to help others? Are you willing to be brought low that others be lifted up? Note that Paul rejoiced at the *privilege* of suffering for the sake of others, because it more closely tied him to the suffering of Jesus.

And We'll Know We Are Christians by Our Suffering

The suffering of the godly is not only a testimony to non-Christians. Because suffering tests the mettle, we find out whether we *really* believe God's promises (see 1 Peter 1:7). But when we do cling to God in spite of our incomprehension and confusion as to why he would afflict us, at the end of it our confidence in God is all the greater. C. S. Lewis pondered this fact when he was struggling through the death of his wife:

> Bridge players tell me that there must be some money on the game "or else people won't take it seriously." Apparently it's like that. Your bid—for God or no God, for a good God or the cosmic sadist, for eternal life or nonentity—will not be serious if nothing much is staked on it. And you will never discover how serious it was until the stakes are raised horribly high; until you find that you are playing not for a counter or for sixpences but for every penny you have in the world. Nothing less will shake a man—or at any rate a man like me—out of his merely verbal thinking and his merely notional beliefs. He has to be knocked silly before he comes to his senses. Only torture will bring out the truth. Only under torture does he discover it himself.[2]

We know that *we* are Christians by our suffering. Remember that Job was tested *because* God approved of him (Job 1). Jesus was severely tested immediately after God uttered his approval of him from heaven (Matt. 3:17). We may be suffering not as punishment but for exactly the opposite reason—because God approves of us.

We must be careful, however. Not all suffering is a sign of God's approval, not all suffering makes us like Christ, and not all those who *think* their suffering is in Christ are actually linked to him. Each person who suffers and claims Christ must examine himself or herself in this regard. In a Philadelphia hospital room lies a young AIDS sufferer who keeps on his wall a picture of Jesus in the Garden of Gethsemane. He says, "I'm there; I'm where Jesus was—I am begging not to have to go through this death." Does the fact that he feels close to Jesus mean that he is? Perhaps it does. Perhaps it does not.

The problem is that human beings can mentally create a "Jesus" after their own image and can hide the real Jesus behind this idol Jesus. Jesus says that not only must a person believe the gospel, but he must repent (Mark 1:15). The question is not whether this man *feels* close to some figure he calls "Jesus" but whether he has repented and identified with the *real* Jesus. Has he recognized his need not just for deliverance from disease and death but for deliverance from sin? Has he submitted to the sovereign lordship of Christ? I do not know the state of this young man's heart. And we must bear in mind that repentance is ordinarily a progressive thing—we usually grow increasingly repentant as we increasingly realize the offensiveness of our sin. But if he has not begun this journey of repentance, then his hope is false, in spite of his suffering.

Fortunately God's grace is great. And often the real Jesus will come and shatter a person's idol Jesus and will enable true repentance.

Sharing the Suffering of Other Believers

Not only does suffering draw the Christian closer to Christ, but it also draws him closer to other Christians. Paul tells us in 1 Corinthians 12:26 that "if one part [of the body] suffers, every part suffers." When others in the church hurt, we hurt. When we hurt, the rest of the church hurts. Further, the experience of suffering enables us to comfort others who are suffering. Before I ever experienced the really intense physical pain of kidney stones, I felt pity for people in pain; afterward I felt *kinship*. I find I have a sense of unity with other people who have experienced it or other similar colic. In 2 Corinthians 1, Paul dwells on this a bit:

> For just as the sufferings of Christ flow over into our lives, so also through Christ our comfort overflows. If we are distressed, it is for your comfort and salvation; if we are comforted, it is for your comfort, which produces in you patient endurance of the same sufferings we suffer. And our hope for you is firm, because we know that just as you share in our sufferings, so also you share in our comfort. (vv. 5–7)

Paul goes on to share some of the sufferings he has endured, and he regards them as beneficial because they compelled him all the more to trust in God. But our point here is this: since Christ comforts him in his affliction, he can comfort them in their affliction. Further, when they suffer, they share in the same comfort he does, which is the identification with Christ's sufferings.

Certainly we all ought to be the same way. I have never been one to express my feelings very openly, and I generally stiffen up around "huggers." But for the couple of months after my father's death, I found that people who ignored my reticent demeanor and hugged me anyway were of tremendous comfort. How much less would our suffering be if we really carried one another's burdens, as the law of Christ commands (Gal. 6:2). When we do identify with others in their sufferings we become even more like Jesus, who "because he endured testing, is able to give aid to those who are presently being tested" (Heb. 2:18 my translation).

For Further Consideration

1. How does the Christian's experience of suffering help her or him bear testimony to Christ?
2. Have you ever been verbally abused because you were a Christian? How did you respond?

3. How can we be sure we are suffering for doing good rather than for doing evil; for the sake of Christ rather than for being irritating, nasty, self-righteous, stuck-up, or stubborn?

4. Have you ever had your faith shaken to its roots by some event? Does this help you relate to other people who have gone through or are going through that experience? Why?

5. Which explanation of Christ's "preaching to the spirits in prison" do you think best fits the passage? How does it help us understand suffering?

6. If we "must through tribulation enter the kingdom of heaven," does this mean if we are not suffering, we are not Christians? Does it mean that if somebody *is* suffering unjustly, he or she must be saved?

7. Have you thought of some ways in which we can share the suffering of other believers?

NOTES

1. The old view that this refers to Christ's preaching the gospel to deceased humans in Hades, in particular to those who died in the flood, has been recently defended by L. Goppelt (*A Commentary on I Peter* [Grand Rapids: Eerdmans, 1993], 255–60). But this whole idea is in conflict both with the context in 1 Peter and with teaching elsewhere in the New Testament. People do not get a "second chance" after death (Heb. 9:27). Further, it is difficult to see how such a digression would be an encouragement to the suffering Christians of Northern Asia Minor, or even of interest to them.

2. C. S. Lewis, *A Grief Observed* (New York: Seabury, 1961), 31–32.

CHAPTER 7

Why Do Christians Suffer? (3)
Training in Righteousness

DISCIPLINE IS NOT a very popular subject. C. S. Lewis pointed out that "we want not so much a father in heaven as a grand-father in heaven—whose plan for the universe was such that it might be said at the end of each day, 'a good time was had by all.' "[1] But God is not a kindly old man; he is a lovingly strict father. Hebrews 12:5–12 tells us that discipline is an indication that we are God's children. God does not bother disciplining the reprobate. This may seem incomprehensible, because non-Christians suffer, too. But only the Christian's suffering can be understood as *discipline*. Without the Holy Spirit who unites a believing sufferer to Christ, suffering only hardens and embitters. The non-Christian's suffering is simply a warning of an even greater judgment to come.

Chastisement

First Peter mentions punishment as a possible cause of suffering, even for a believer, in 2:20 (a slave might be punished for wrongdoing) and in 1 Corinthians 11, Paul mentions that some have died because they were abusing the Lord's Supper. But there is nothing noteworthy about suffering as punishment for wicked behavior. Such suffering is expected and just. One reason for suffering is the natural consequence of sin. If you steal, you may suffer in jail. If you are sexually immoral, you might get AIDS.

Caryn had driven her car to the party, but she was having such a good time with her boyfriend that she did not want to drive home. She gave her keys to another friend, Jim, and asked him to drive so that she could sit on her boyfriend's lap on the way home. Coming down a hill too fast, Jim lost control of the car and crashed into the side of a building. Everyone but Caryn had a seat belt on and was only slightly injured, but Caryn, sitting on her boyfriend's lap with no seat belt on, was thrown from the car and shattered her tail bone. For two weeks she lay in the hospital in intense pain. Caryn acted foolishly and irresponsibly, and suffered for it.

So did Jim, the driver. Caryn fully recovered and became the star of her field hockey team, but two years later she sued Jim for medical expenses, plus the pain and suffering she experienced those two weeks, plus possible future pain and suffering, and won a sizable judgment on all three requests. Caryn ended up being nicely rewarded for her foolishness. But the world in general is usually not so rewarding of it. God created the universe in such a way that foolish, irresponsible, and/or immoral behavior will eventually result in suffering. And only rarely is such suffering compensated.

This is true for Christian and non-Christian alike. But even here there is a difference between the suffering of the believer and that of the nonbeliever, because the believer knows that the total and true penalty for his or her sinful behavior has already been carried by Christ. Further, there is a difference in the way believers and nonbelievers respond to the painful consequences of sinful acts. A believer who is sensitive to the Holy Spirit will see the connection between cause and effect, and although it may take a long time, a Christian will repent of the causative sin and accept the responsibility.

A believer who suffered because of his sin can be seen in Psalm 32:3–5. Note how for a long time he resisted acknowledging his sin, but suffering eventually led to his repentance:

> When I kept silent,
>   my bones wasted away
>   through my groaning all day long.
> For day and night
>   your hand was heavy upon me;
> my strength was sapped
>   as in the heat of summer.
> Then I acknowledged my sin to you
>   and did not cover up my iniquity.
> I said, "I will confess
>   my transgressions to the LORD"—
> and you forgave
>   the guilt of my sin.

God frequently disciplines his children to enable them to acknowledge their sin. But the unbeliever, or even a believer who is resisting the Spirit, will often shift the blame onto someone or something else, even when it is obvious that the person has caused his or her own suffering. (They may even, like Caryn, sometimes get away with it for a while.) This blame shifting is evident, for example, with unrepentant AIDS sufferers who contracted the disease by promiscuous homosexual behavior. We should not pick on AIDS sufferers too much, since not all acquired it through promiscuity, and even those who did are not inherently greater sinners than any of us. But it is tragic that some AIDS sufferers have become hardened to the point where they are furious, not with themselves, or even the "lover" from whom they acquired the disease. They are angry at their parents for not loving them unconditionally, or they are angry at God for creating such an unfairly selective disease, or they are angry at society for "forcing" them into promiscuity because of the ostracism of homosexuality. And anyone who dares point out the obvious causal link between their contracting HIV and their sexual behavior is met with violent accusations of "homophobia."

I suspect it may be unusually difficult for homosexuals to repent in today's atmosphere, because they have invested so much effort into justifying their lifestyle and have adopted a culture that has justified it. To repent under these circumstances means to throw over all that effort and to relinquish the very culture that has been supportive and met their social and emotional needs. Only where another social environment stands ready to meet those needs is a homosexual likely to be able to repent, and the church has in the past typically not been ready to provide that environment for gays and lesbians.

Further, recognizing responsibility for one's own condition takes a long time and involves many stages, and people with AIDS usually do not have a long time. Repentance is usually not an instantaneous thing but a progressively developing attitude. Most believers do not *first* fully repent of their sins and *then* begin their life of faith—they begin their life of faith in Christ and therefore also begin to repent of their sins. And as we grow in Christ we become increasingly aware of our need for repentance.

This means that we are obligated to show compassion even to those who suffer for their own sins. God brought affliction upon his own people for their sin, but he still had compassion on them. All Christians in this life are still susceptible to sin. And God, like a parent who punishes his children, sometimes inflicts suffering on his children because they have done wrong. Such suffering is not simple retribution. There is such a thing as a retributive punishment for unbelievers (1 Thess. 2:16; Rev. 20; etc.), and this retributive suffering is totally fair; it exactly fits the wickedness it retributes. But when God's children suffer for wrongdoing, it is *restorative*. We sometimes call it "chastisement" because it is a purging kind of punishment. In fact, it appears God is much more diligent about punishing *in this life* his own children than non-Christians for sin. Remember Hebrews 12:7–8: God is treating you as sons; and if you are not disciplined, then you must be illegitimate.

Discipline is also a theme in Revelation. The book of Revelation seems to most Christians like a fascinating but altogether mysterious book, full of strange symbolism and difficult prophecies. But Revelation was actually intended to be quite practical, and its opening chapters, though indeed full of symbols and metaphors, are a clear rebuke to many of the churches of Asia Minor.

In Revelation 3:19 the Lord says, "Those whom I love I rebuke and discipline." The context in Revelation 3 is dealing at least partly with the necessity of suffering. The church in Laodicea had been seeking to avoid suffering by compromising. They were tepid Christians (3:16). Jesus tells them therefore to "buy from me gold refined in the fire . . ." (v. 17). Gold "refined in the fire" is a metaphor for the character produced by suffering (1 Peter 1:7). Jesus wanted the church of Laodicea to accept his discipline.

The problem is that punishment, even when it is chastisement for our good, is never easy to take, because it means acknowledging that we have done wrong. But chastisement does no good until we admit we did something wrong, and so it is altogether appropriate when we suffer to ask first, "Is this the consequence of some sin on my part?" If it is, we should stop doing that sin right away, and we ought to be *thankful* that God does not let us get away with sin. On the other hand, we ought to be careful that we do not blame ourselves simply because we are suffering. Chastisement is not the only reason for suffering.

A Wake-up Call

Kim Gallagher, who went to the same high school my daughter attended, is a two-time Olympic medalist in the 800 meter run. Today, at age 33, she has a seven-year-old daughter, and she is dying of stomach cancer. She does not profess to understand why she has cancer, but she does say, "The cancer was my calling back to a higher power. The only way I could even slightly help myself was to give it to God and let him work with it."[2]

Sometimes suffering is discipline not for something *in particular* that we have done wrong, but a means of waking us up from our lethargy and lack of concern for God, which is certainly a sinful attitude. Nehemiah prayed, "Therefore thou didst give them into the hand of their enemies, who made them suffer; and in the time of their suffering they cried to thee and thou didst hear them from heaven; and according to thy great mercies thou didst give them saviors who saved them from the hand of their enemies" (Neh. 9:27 RSV). The suffering of the Israelites made them wake up to their responsibility to God. It was their fathers who had sinned, but the children are the ones awakened by suffering.

There are many examples in Scripture of suffering being a means of spiritual awakening. For example, the piling up of seeming misfortunes led Reuben and the other brothers eventually to repent of their mistreatment of Joseph. You can read the story in Genesis 42–44.

C. S. Lewis made the observation that God whispers in our pleasures but shouts in our pains. "Pain is his megaphone to rouse a dulled world."[3] And we need a megaphone in our ears. One of our problems as fallen human beings is our reluctance to face our own need. My friend who works with HIV patients tells me that when someone first learns he or she is HIV positive, usually the first response is shock, followed by denial. People generally do not deal spiritually with their condition until AIDS sets in and they begin to feel the pain of it. God sometimes uses suffering because it takes pain to tenderize the hardened conscience. Believers can become almost as insensitive to God's voice as unbelievers, but it is hard to ignore suffering. As Richard Baxter observed, "Suffering so unbolts the door of the heart that the Word hath easier entrance."[4]

We should point out, however, that suffering *by itself* does not lead to repentance or spiritual awakening. Much as in the case of death, people generally react to suffering in phases—shock, denial, rebellion, anger, depression, shame, and withdrawal. Genuine repentance is not produced by natural causes—it is a supernatural work of the Holy Spirit. And even for the Christian, repentance takes time, and Christians may go through these same phases. But the Christian, the one who really knows God, will always keep coming back to the problem of God. Thinking about God and crying out to him are what eventually will turn the heart to self-examination and open up the soul to recognition of need. As the psalmist cried out,

> Search me, O God, and know my heart;
>   test me and know my anxious thoughts.
> See if there is any offensive way in me,
>   and lead me in the way everlasting. (Ps. 139:23–24)

Conversely, for people who have assumed they are Christians but have not really submitted personally to God, who are not sustained by the Holy Spirit, suffering only makes it clear that their belief was only on the surface.

Similarly, suffering can either draw people together or drive them apart. Stanley Hauerwas noted in his book *Naming the Silences*[5] that suffering in general isolates a person, because most suffering is unique and not completely like anyone else's. As Jeremiah cried out, "Is any suffering like my suffering?" (Lam. 1:12). Condolences from others who have not experienced the same kind of suffering can sometimes make things worse. It is rather strange, that when we endure suffering, we both yearn for condolence and dread it at the same time. But although suffering may isolate, it can also draw together. People who are suffering the same thing often draw together, as we see in the case of catastrophes. If our suffering is in Christ, then even if it is in some ways unique, it is suffering *in Christ,* and so is like the sufferings of others *in Christ.* Such suffering draws us together with him and also draws us closer to others who suffer and helps us understand them.

My grandmother died very horribly of breast cancer when my father was only sixteen. At the time she died, my grandfather was out getting drunk, leaving my father alone to watch his mother die. Very late in his life, Dad was able to tell me that his hatred of his father for abandoning his mother in the hour of her need (and his) continued for many years, even after his father's death. But when he was in his fifties, Dad himself contracted cancer. In his own suffering, Dad began to think about God's demands more seriously, and eventually he was able to forgive his father. Dad finally understood that his father was out getting drunk because he himself was suffering, too, and did not have the spiritual resources to handle it. Suffering without God only made my grandfather into an alcoholic. My dad's suffering was a tool the Holy Spirit used to enable him first to understand Jesus' suffering and then to sympathize with his father's suffering. Cancer was his wake-up call, just as it was for Kim Gallagher.

Keeping Alert

The pilot guides his aircraft down into the murk, fully alert as he tries to land on IFR (Instrument Flight Rules). The windows might as well not be there. Flying blind, he is totally dependent on his instruments and the signals from the control tower. Check altimeter, check air speed, check flaps, check yaw and pitch, check all navigation indicators, check radar, check check check check. Suddenly the air clears, and there is the runway immediately beneath the plane. The landing is safe.

On another beautiful clear day a pilot comes in for a landing on VFR (Visual Flight Rules), and he stops paying attention to what he is doing, because it is so easy when you can *see*. As a result, he comes in a bit too fast and gets a bit roughed up. The apparent ease of VFR made the pilot a little sleepy when he should still have been alert.

The same is true of our spiritual lives. God sometimes sends a little murk so that we will pay closer attention to the way we are flying. But he has also provided very accurate instruments, namely Scripture and prayer. Note how *dependent* the great apostle to the Gentiles was, because God let Satan torment him.

> To keep me from becoming conceited because of these surpassingly great revelations, there was given me a thorn in my flesh, a messenger of Satan, to torment me. Three times I pleaded with the Lord to take it away from me. But he said to me, "My grace is sufficient for you, for my power is made perfect in weakness." Therefore I will boast all the more gladly about my weaknesses, so that Christ's power may rest on me.

That is why, for Christ's sake, I delight in weaknesses,
in insults, in hardships, in persecutions, in difficulties.
For when I am weak, then I am strong. (2 Cor. 12:7–10)

Paul had not committed some sin that deserved this "thorn
in the flesh." God allowed Satan to afflict him solely to keep
Paul from getting conceited and forgetting on whom he must
depend. As sad as it is to say, we too need some suffering or
we slide off into apathy or pride. Thanks be to God that he
keeps us alert, even if he must send suffering.

For Further Consideration

1. Is all suffering discipline? If not, what distinguishes suffering as discipline from other types of suffering?
2. In your own experience, did you first become aware of
   your sin, repent, and then believe in Christ, or did you
   first believe in Christ, and then discover your need of
   repentance? If the latter, how do you understand what
   took place?
3. Has God ever sent something into your life to rouse you
   from spiritual lethargy? Did it work?
4. Have you ever felt resentment that God keeps you dependent on him? Why did you feel this way?
5. How can we minister to sufferers such as the AIDS victims
   who are struggling with acknowledging their own sin? How
   can we both refuse to condone their sin and at the same
   time provide an atmosphere of acceptance and support?

NOTES
1. C. S. Lewis, *The Problem of Pain* (New York: Macmillan, 1962), 39.
2. The story of Kim Gallagher's cancer was reported by Elliott Almond,
   "Battling stomach cancer, she's in another kind of race," *Los Ange-
   les Times*, republished in *Philadelphia Inquirer*, June 13, 1995.

3. Lewis, *The Problem of Pain*, 93.
4. R. Baxter, *The Saints' Everlasting Rest* (repr. Grand Rapids: Baker, 1978), 246.
5. S. Hauerwas, *Naming the Silences* (Grand Rapids: Eerdmans, 1990).

CHAPTER 8

Why Do Christians Suffer? (4) Getting Ready for Glory

FIRST PETER 1:6–7 makes the strange claim that we ought to rejoice in sufferings:

> In this you greatly rejoice, though now for a little while you may have had to suffer grief in all kinds of trials. These have come so that your faith—of greater worth than gold, which perishes even though refined by fire—may be proved genuine and may result in praise, glory and honor when Jesus Christ is revealed.

How can anyone *rejoice* in sufferings? I do not fully understand how this can be possible, but we can point out that Peter does not say we should rejoice *at* the sufferings. We are not told to become masochists. Rather, we rejoice because the sufferings are being used for our benefit, and our knowledge that God is showing us to be *approved* enables us to have a certain kind of joy. Remember that Job and Jesus himself were tested because God approved of them.

Later, Peter refers to the "fiery ordeal" that his readers are facing (4:12 NASB). What is the function of such testing by ordeal? Is it, as James Crenshaw suggests, a means of God's obtaining "a certain kind of knowledge which he lacks, that is, precisely how men and women will act in trying circumstances"?[1] Does God need to test us to find out if, as free human beings, we will decide for the right even when the going gets rough?

No—there is no suggestion in 1 Peter that God does not know what we are and therefore must test us to find out. Rather it is we who do not know what we are and therefore must be tested. Like the athlete whose coach continues to press him to break his own records, in order that the athlete may see for himself just how far he can go, so we are pressed in order that we may know ourselves.

Testing also connects us to Jesus Christ. Note how Christians as "living stones" are connected to Jesus the chosen precious cornerstone in 1 Peter 2:6. Peter is quoting from Isaiah 28:16, where the original word is not "chosen" but "tested." Certainly God did not need to test Jesus to find out what Jesus' character was, but the testing did show the world what Jesus' character was.

Peter might also have had in mind something of what was ultimately demonstrated by Job. God may be showing the spiritual universe what a glorious thing he has created in his people in Jesus Christ—showing the angels and perhaps even Satan how his grace has been effective in our lives (cf. Eph. 3:10).

But whether or not the spirit world is here in view, 1 Peter 1:7 indicates that the very proof or testing of faith is precious. Although it is not apparent from the translation above, grammatically, it is not the faith itself that is precious, although the testing does demonstrate its quality, but rather the *proof* of the faith that is precious. The testing is the means of demonstrating that our faith is valid and genuine. It is therefore something to rejoice in (1:6). Suffering is always grievous, and the point is not that we should somehow take pleasure in pain, but that we should see the *purpose* of suffering in proving to us the ground and genuineness of our relationship to Jesus Christ. It is the power of God that enables (v. 5).

It also means that we do not shirk when we are called on to suffer. Jack Kevorkian could not be in business unless there were people who thought the way to deal with pain is to avoid it—at all costs. This option is not open to the Christian. It is only by accepting discipline that we can truly identify with Christ, because he is the suffering one. It is "the one who overcomes," that is, the one who endures suffering in Christ, who will sit with Jesus on the throne (Rev. 3:21). This, by the way, is the context for Jesus' great invitation "Here I am! I stand at the door and knock. If anyone hears my voice and opens the door, I will come in and eat with him and he with me" (v. 20). This is not primarily an invitation to become a Christian. It is an invitation to the Christian to be willing to so thoroughly identify with Jesus as to be willing to share in Christ's sufferings, and so become an "overcomer."

But what if we fail? What if we respond to suffering by cursing God and withdrawing from him? Surely we cannot then regard the proof of our *lack* of faith as precious. Even here however we can be grateful that testing has shown our faith to be weak, because it shows us again our weakness and dependence on God's grace and mercy, and if we really know the Lord Jesus, the failure itself will drive us to him for forgiveness. Remember that Peter himself, who tells us that the proof of our faith is precious, knew what it was like to fail the test. He responded to Jesus' arrest by cursing God and withdrawing from him.[2] But after Jesus forgave him, he became all the more passionate in his gratitude and love.

This process of testing, Peter compares to refining. Gold is tested by fire, and its value is thereby proven. Likewise the proof of faith is more precious than gold that perishes, and it too is tested by the fire of suffering. Gold is the least perishable of earthly metals, but since it is of this world, even it is ultimately perishable. Faith—genuine, tested faith—is not. But just as gold is not only proven but *refined* by fire, so is faith purified by suffering.

Purification

We gladly subject extremely valuable gold-bearing rocks to intense fire in order to separate the gold from the worthless rock. So too, God is willing to expose us to suffering in order, as the hymn writer says, "thy dross to consume and thy gold to refine." Again, it is not easy to endure, because some of that dross looks rather precious to us, and it hurts to have it consumed. Furthermore, we often do not see any point at all to the suffering. We ourselves may see no good effects.

I once heard a story about a little girl who developed a fever that became dangerously high. To keep her from brain damage, her parents had to put her into a cold bath, which to the child felt like ice. The little girl could not understand why her parents were torturing her that way. Was she being punished for something bad? If not, why were Mommy and Daddy doing this? She did not understand, nor could her parents explain it to her, but it was still necessary to get rid of an evil in her body.

C. S. Lewis wrote, "Suppose that what you are up against is a surgeon whose intentions are wholly good. The kinder and more conscientious he is, the more inexorably he will go on cutting."[3] Lewis illustrated this well in the *Voyage of the Dawn Treader* where the nasty little boy Eustace, now trapped inside a symbolically appropriate dragon's body, must let Aslan the lion remove his draconian carcass with a huge claw.

What enables him to endure it is the love on Aslan's face as he does the surgery. How marvelous to remember that God is not only the kindly surgeon; he himself has been under the knife. As T. S. Eliot said, "The wounded surgeon plies the steel that questions the distempered part."[4]

Suffering is, according to Peter, something like a trial by fire (1 Peter 1:7; 4:12). Fire purifies gold, but it consumes rubbish (including tinsel!). Christians endure the fire because it burns off that part of us that is not glorious. A lump of gold-bearing rock is just as dull and shapeless as any other rock, but the pure gold that is left after the fire is beautiful and precious. How does this happen? It happens because suffering administered by the Holy Spirit purges our old sinful nature, the selfish *me* who wants to be the center of the universe. As this selfish *me* is progressively killed off by suffering, it allows the Spirit of Jesus within us to be more manifest. Paul says in 2 Corinthians 4:11, "For we who are alive are always being given over to death for Jesus' sake, so that his life may be revealed in our mortal body." Such dying daily (1 Cor. 15:31) is certainly unpleasant; but it is necessary.

Weaning from the World

The story of the Exodus in the book by that name gives us the paradigm for this facet of suffering. God saw the suffering of his people (Exod. 3:7) and then delivered them. But why did he allow the suffering to happen in the first place? Could he not rather have simply prevented it?

If he had done so, would the Israelites have ever desired to leave Egypt? It was hard enough to get them to leave even when they were suffering. Likewise it is hard enough for us to leave aside the treasures of this evil world even though we suffer in it. How much harder is it for us to desire the new heavens and new earth when our lives here are comfortable?

As Augustine pointed out, we get things backward. We are supposed to rejoice in God and in his image bearers (people) and use things of the world. We prefer to use God and people and rejoice in the things of the world. Suffering weans us from such foolish notions. Joni Eareckson is vibrant and energetic, but bottled up inside a body that will do little she wants it to. It is hard for her to rejoice much in the things of this world. She says she really *yearns* for the future inheritance—a restored body. Actually, Joni says she yearns even more for her total deliverance from sin. I suspect that the fact that she has her eyes set so firmly on the future is why she not only does not sink into self pity but is able to be used by the Lord so effectively.

James Dobson, in his *Focus on the Family* series, recounts the story of a terminally ill little boy who would from time to time cry out, "I hear the bells." His nurses at first thought he was hallucinating. Later his mother explained, "I told him that when the pain got bad to remember that God was starting to ring the bells welcoming him to heaven." There is nothing like pain to make a true believer turn away from this age and focus more surely on the age to come.

I think this could be one reason why God is allowing this case of the four-year-old's abduction by judge to happen. For me, at least, it is a strong-dosage reminder that the United States, for all its benefits and liberties (which are now being seriously eroded), is still *enemy territory*—we are still not home here, and we dare not get too comfortable. As 1 Peter puts it, we are *aliens and strangers*. This is not our homeland.

Preparation for glory

When Peter discusses suffering as testing, he puts it in the context of preparing the Christian for an eternal inheritance. Let's look again at this passage:

In this you greatly rejoice, though now for a little while you may have had to suffer grief in all kinds of trials. These have come so that your faith—of greater worth than gold, which perishes even though refined by fire—may be proved genuine and may result in praise, glory and honor when Jesus Christ is revealed. Though you have not seen him, you love him; and even though you do not see him now, you believe in him and are filled with an inexpressible and glorious joy, for you are receiving the goal of your faith, the salvation of your souls. (1 Peter 1:6–9)

This is related to the weaning purpose of suffering, but the emphasis is on the fact that suffering prepares us for the weight of glory. Paul says something similar in 2 Corinthians 4:17–18.

For our light and momentary troubles are achieving for us an eternal glory that far outweighs them all. So we fix our eyes not on what is seen, but on what is unseen. For what is seen is temporary, but what is unseen is eternal.

What we see is suffering. What is unseen is glory. Notice that Paul does not ignore or deny the reality of the present (visible) sufferings, but he does understand the visible present sufferings in the light of the invisible future glory. To trust God is to act on what you know by his word, though you do not see.

We actually do this in our daily lives all the time. When we get up enough courage to go to the dentist and we sit in the ugly chair that looks as if it were taken from a torture chamber, what we *see* are various instruments of torture (drills, picks, needles, interrogation light, etc.). But we know by other means that the pain we are approaching is ultimately for our good. The trust we give to the faithful Creator (1 Peter 4:19) is even more sensible, even when we face the destruction of our bodies. Remember Job's words: Though he slay me, yet will I hope in him. Paul goes on:

> Now we know that if the earthly tent we live in is destroyed, we have a building from God, an eternal house in heaven, not built by human hands. Meanwhile we groan, longing to be clothed with our heavenly dwelling, because when we are clothed, we will not be found naked. For while we are in this tent, we groan and are burdened, because we do not wish to be unclothed but to be clothed with our heavenly dwelling, so that what is mortal may be swallowed up by life. Now it is God who has made us for this very purpose and has given us the Spirit as a deposit, guaranteeing what is to come. (2 Cor. 5:1–5)

The winter of 1994 was memorable in the Eastern United States for its ice storms. Trees became coated with layers of ice, which sometimes would cause branches to break off. Some trees, especially those which grew in more or less sheltered areas, did not survive. But trees that had been more exposed to winds and storms stood up. And those that did stand up were positively glorious in their weight of ice. Adversity prepared those trees for their weight of glory. If we have not been prepared by adversity for our weight of glory, how are we going to hold up under it?

> If we are children, then we are heirs, co-heirs with Christ, as we are suffering in union with him with the result that we may be glorified in union with him. For I reckon that the sufferings we undergo now are

not worth comparing to the glory which is going to be revealed in us. (Rom. 8:17–18 my translation)

There is in life a priority of some things over others. Therefore the good of the more important things takes precedence over the good of less important things. For example, we should sometimes forego the pleasure of eating a candy bar (a momentary good) for the greater good of the health of the whole body. Sometimes we may even make our bodies "suffer" by hard exercising, for the same greater end. Is it not appropriate that we forego the good of a pain-free life now for the greater good of the eternal weight of glory? It is fortunate we do not have a choice in the matter, because we probably would choose a pain-free life now and forego the future glory (even as sometimes we avoid going to a dentist when we know we should), but our Father does not see it that way, any more than conscientious earthly parents see things the way their children do.

Paul in Romans 5:3–5 explains this in terms of character building:

> Not only so, but we also rejoice in our sufferings, because we know that suffering produces perseverance; perseverance, character; and character, hope. And hope does not disappoint us, because God has poured out his love into our hearts by the Holy Spirit, whom he has given us.

All these positive effects of suffering assume that the sufferer relates his suffering to his relationship with God through Christ. Unless a sufferer is clinging to Christ, he or she is not going to persevere and will not develop the character of Jesus but will abandon hope, even as Elie Wiesel did. And even if some should somehow persevere and continue to hope in someone or something other than Jesus, their hopes sooner or later *will* disappoint, because they will not have the love of God poured into their hearts by the Holy Spirit. As we saw in the first part of this chapter, Christ is the primary focus of the meaning of the believer's suffering. The suffering of Christ has linked him to us, and our suffering in turn links us to him. It is only in Christ that Christian suffering has its true meaning.

For Further Consideration

1. Have you ever met someone who has suffered a great deal and yet is full of joy? How do you explain this?
2. Why is it important that we be "weaned from the world"? Isn't the world God's creation? Is it not therefore good?
3. How much at home do you feel in this world? If you have suffered, has the suffering made you more ready for your eternal home? How?
4. List some other ways in which we operate by trust rather than by sight? Since we do this, what makes it so extraordinarily difficult sometimes to trust God?

NOTES

1. James Crenshaw, *A Whirlpool of Torment: Israelite Traditions of God as an Oppressive Presence* (Philadelphia: Fortress, 1984), 2.
2. This is one of the few events recorded in all four Gospels (Matt. 26:69–75; Mark 14:66–72; Luke 22:54–71; John 18:25–27). It clearly made a powerful impression on the early church that the first great spokesman for Christianity, who rejoiced to suffer for Christ's sake (Acts 5:41), had earlier failed so miserably.
3. C. S. Lewis, *A Grief Observed* (New York: Seabury, 1961), 36.
4. T. S. Eliot, "East Coker," in *The Complete Poems and Plays, 1909–1950* (New York: Harcourt, Brace & Company, 1952), 123–29.

CHAPTER 9

How Should We Then Suffer?

IT IS ALL VERY WELL for us to theorize about why Christians suffer. But when we ourselves are actually going through suffering, the theory seems awfully remote and hard to hold on to. My experience of intense pain reduced me to a state of frantic flapping around like a fish out of water, trying to find some way, anyway, to get the pain to stop. I think I am not unique in this response. Thus we not only need to try to understand the "why" of suffering, which sometimes remains not fully answered anyway; we also need to ask "how" we should suffer. On the other hand, neither can we answer the "how" without relating to the "why." We are not looking for some kind of stoic ability to ignore suffering; we want to understand the meaning. Somehow we need to keep both the "why" and the "how" of suffering in mind. This chapter will try to answer the "how" of suffering in relation to the "why."

Called to Suffer

Suffering, for the Christian, is a vocation—we are called to suffer. A popular evangelistic tract refers to the "abundant life" enjoyed by the Christian. This method sometimes gives the impression that the Christian life is inherently more pleasant than the non-Christian life. But the number of passages that speak about the Christian as a *sufferer* suggests that this may not be a totally honest approach—indeed we ought to expect the Christian life to be *less* pleasant, at least with respect to outward circumstances. In Acts 14:22 Paul says that it is "through many tribulations that we must enter the Kingdom of God" (NASB). The New Testament is rather consistent in this: Romans 8:17; 1 Corinthians 12:26; Philippians 1:29–30; 1 Thessalonians 2:14; 2 Timothy 3:12; 1 Peter 3:14; and 5:1 all indicate that Christians are called by God to suffer as part and parcel of the Christian life. Suffering therefore is a *privilege* and a sign of election (Matt. 5:12; Acts 5:41; 1 Cor. 11:32; 2 Cor. 6:4–5; Gal. 3:4; Col. 1:29; 2 Thess. 1:4–8; 1 Peter 4:12–19). First Peter even calls suffering for Jesus' sake a sign of "favor" with God (1 Peter 2:19–21 NASB). The Christian life is no joy ride.

We are not, however, called to be gloomy. The joy of the gospel ought to have its way, even in our sufferings. Nor are we called to make ourselves suffer or to seek to suffer. Some Christians have from time to time thought that self-imposed suffering helps to purge the body of sinfulness, but Colossians 2:20–23 makes it clear that, although such suffering may look helpful, it is of no real value. In fact, self-induced suffering feeds pride and self-righteousness.

Our calling is rather *to endure suffering in a certain way*. As 1 Peter says, we should suffer as a Christian (4:16). This is because Christ was called to suffer and did so in a certain way. Christ did not *like* suffering; he did not seek the suffering itself; in fact, he even prayed it would pass him by. But he did not shirk it, and he also knew it to be necessary. As soon as the disciples began to recognize who Jesus really was, Jesus started telling them that he *must* go to Jerusalem, suffer, die, and be raised (see Mark 8:34; etc.). Up to the very end, the disciples resisted this idea, but Jesus pointed out that if he did not die (Matt. 26:54), "how then would the Scriptures be fulfilled that say it must happen in this way?" Jesus' way to the kingdom of God was through suffering, the *via dolorosa*. Is it so surprising then that the way we must take to arrive at the kingdom of God is through suffering? And yet we seem to be surprised when suffering comes. Which is probably why 1 Peter must remind us, "Do not be surprised at the painful trial you are suffering, as though something strange were happening to you" (4:12).

Resisting Oppression?

It is by bearing these two things in mind—that we are called to suffer but are not to make ourselves suffer—that I think we can answer the question, "To what degree should we *resist* suffering when it is imposed upon us? Are we passively to accept our oppression, or are we to rebel against it?" The answer is, neither. We are obligated to submit to the hand of God, and insofar as he places authority over us, we must submit to it (1 Peter 2:13–20). But we are not required to submit to oppression that is not from a proper authority.

Again Jesus' attitude is instructive. He did not allow himself to be manipulated or destroyed by a riotous crowd (Luke 4:28–30). But neither did he use force to prevent his suffering, when it came about by the duly constituted authorities, as depraved and godless as those authorities were.

> When they hurled their insults at him, he did not retaliate; when he suffered, he made no threats. Instead, he entrusted himself to him who judges justly. (1 Peter 2:23)

Peter mentions this when he discusses how slaves should submit to their masters, even unfair and harsh ones. Slavery is not something God established, any more than Roman imperialism is something God commanded, but it is a form of human social authority structure. And the same pattern is advised to every suffering Christian (4:19). It is God who will repay (4:18). This is not exactly *passive*, because the believer should be actively crying out to God for deliverance, but neither does it attempt to do God's work of judgment for him.

This, like the subject of discipline, is *extremely* unpopular today and no doubt will make some people angry. Nobody wishes to be a "doormat." Books are written to show how 1 Peter and other passages do not mean what they appear to mean, and that really we should resist oppression. Of course, plenty of Old Testament passages talk about overcoming oppression, but they are speaking of our responsibility to alleviate the oppression of *others*, not to resist by force or violence our own oppression. Jesus did not allow himself to be used as a doormat either—he never let his oppressors set the agenda—but neither did he fight violence with violence. This is what we must do; we must humble ourselves under the mighty hand of God. The non-Christians of the world, who do not trust in the faithful Creator, will try to resolve their oppression by taking matters into their own hands. But the fact that we are *called* to suffer as *Christians*, and have our focus primarily on the future, should mean a radical change in our attitude toward suffering.

Suffering as Jesus Did

What is this "certain way" that we are called to suffer? Above all it is, as we mentioned earlier, suffering *in Christ*. It does no good to try to bear our suffering ourselves; we must cling to Christ. That sounds easy enough when you are not suffering. But it is not so easy when you are actually suffering. How can I respond to God when he appears to be abusing me?

Peter has told us that Jesus left us an example (1 Peter 2:21). And how did Jesus respond to God when he appeared to be abusing him? He prayed honestly, and he prayed using the Psalms. He forthrightly tells God in Gethsemane, "I do not want to go through with this," although he is also able to say, "Nevertheless, not what I want, but what you want." And at the apex of his grief, abandonment, and pain on the most devilish instrument of torture the ancient world had devised, Jesus cried out, "My God, my God, why have you forsaken me." This is no pious utterance; it is a cry of anguish. It is not a request for an intellectual, theological answer explaining the necessity for the atoning death—Jesus knew that already. It was rather a cry from the heart, using the very words of the Psalms. The Psalms were Jesus' resource in time of suffering. If we are going to suffer *in Christ*, we ought to respond the way he did, by the Psalms. And the Psalms are apt. No other body of literature in the world so completely runs the range of human feelings. The Psalms are not just expressions of joy, elation, trust, thanks, and hope; they also express anguish, despair, anger, pain, confusion, and sorrow to the dregs.

Praying the Psalms

Thank God he gave us the Psalms. Many of them deal with the child of God suffering and crying out to God. There is even a special class of psalms that scholars refer to as "psalms of lament," which sometimes have a special metrical form distinct from other psalms.[1] Just a quick look at the psalter shows that Psalms 4–7; 10–13; 22; 25; 28; 42–43; 55–57; 59–60; 64; 69–70; 74; 77; 79; 86; 88; 102; 123; 130; 137; and 140–43 all cry out to God in distress. We also have great poems and prayers that are like psalms in Jeremiah, Lamentations (especially), Isaiah, Ezekiel, Daniel, Habakkuk, and many other places. In addition there are also a number of psalms of thanksgiving in which the psalmist *was* in difficulty but God delivered him from suffering (9; 18; 30; etc.).

What do we learn from these prayers in the Psalms? First, we find total honesty. We sometimes get really mad at God—and it does no good to hide the fact. We must face reality. Unfairness is rampant—and we sense its wrongness. Trying to extinguish this anger and sense of wrongness is not Christian piety; it is Stoicism or Buddhism. And even if God had not given us the Psalms and the example of Jesus, we certainly could not fool him who looks upon the heart.

The second lesson is that such honest crying out to God is in fact an expression of faith. It is just at these worst of times that God seems most silent. "The heavens are like brass" at times. As we saw earlier, in Psalm 88, the psalmist never resolves to an expression of hope the way the other lament psalms do. But his very crying out is still an expression of faith. Job remained faithful, God says, even though his own despair at times was very deep. When you are suffering so much that you cannot with easy confidence say, "I trust you, God," this psalm is a great gift. It is a reminder that faith can be hidden and yet still be genuine.

Third, they remind us that God is still God. With the exception of Psalm 88, all the psalms of lament have a turning point, where the psalmist shifts from his despair to his voice of confidence in God. Sorrow is transformed, not into happiness, but into a confident, joyful hope. This is what makes these psalms of such comfort in times of distress. As we read, we can, like the psalmist, move from despair to hope, from distrust to confidence, and from agitation to repose as we remember who God is.

All of these psalms I named earlier can be of great comfort

to the sufferer. In the next chapter I am going to focus on six psalms in particular, focusing on faith (13; 27), hope (22; 42), and love (73; 131). But before we look at these psalms, we need to point out that we do so in union with Christ and as part of his body the church, not because we by ourselves have any claim on God.

Sharing Christ's Suffering by the Psalms

The Psalms are very inspiring literature and have been of great comfort to many people because they are so expressive of the human predicament. But what makes the Psalms especially important for Christians is that Christ prayed these Psalms. Some of the Psalms are clearly stated in the New Testament to be about Christ. Some of them Christ himself uttered (most notably Ps. 22 on the cross). But since he teaches his disciples in Luke 24:44–47 that the Law, the Prophets, and *the Psalms* are about him, we ought to understand all the Psalms as in some way related to him. If we are *in Christ*, if we are covenantally linked to him, then we can also pray these psalms. This is how we are to suffer as Christ did, by praying these psalms as expressions of our own faith, hope, and love.

For Further Consideration

1. What does it mean that Christians are "called to suffer"?
2. Why did the ascetic hermits of the early church try to make themselves suffer? Do you think their efforts were misguided? Why? Have you ever tried to make yourself suffer? Was it a good or helpful thing to do?
3. What are the three lessons we learn from the Psalms about how to suffer? Why is it important to remember these things?

4. What should you do if you are oppressed by other people? Is it right to resist oppression? If so, under what circumstances?
5. What methods are appropriate in overcoming the oppression of other people? For example, is it right to block access to abortion clinics?

NOTE

1. For more on the lament psalms, see Tremper Longman III, "Lament," in *Cracking Old Testament Codes*, ed. D. Brent Sandy and R. L. Giese, Jr. (Nashville: Broadman and Holman, 1995), 197–215.

CHAPTER 10

Psalms for Sufferers

PHILIP YANCEY NOTES that there are three things that greatly increase suffering: fear, hopelessness, and loneliness.[1] Fear can magnify pain in the mind to the point where it becomes intolerable—not because the pain is itself unendurable, but because fear is so devastating to the mind. Hopelessness makes a person "give up" and cease to struggle, greatly magnifying the suffering, as in the case of Elie Wiesel when his father died. Loneliness, even without other suffering, is misery; and when we are suffering, the loneliness exacerbates every weakness because the mind as well as the body is in pain. "Who suffers alone suffers most in the mind."[2] Further, suffering often increases loneliness because healthy people do not like to go to hospitals and be reminded of their own vulnerability. Suffering sometimes carries stigma too. Every age has certain diseases that are stigmatized, that people do not talk about. A hundred years ago, mental illness bore that stigma. Today it is AIDS. Suffering becomes shameful.

Paul said in 1 Corinthians 13 that three things endure: faith, hope, love. It is precisely these that conquer fear, hope-

lessness, loneliness. In this chapter we will look at six psalms
that demonstrate faith conquering fear, hope banishing hopelessness, and love overcoming loneliness.

Faith Conquers Fear

Psalm 13 is an example of how the psalmist's trust in God
eventually overcomes his confusion and dismay at God's inaction. His cry at the beginning is a cry every sufferer shouts
repeatedly: "How long, O Lord!"

> How long, O LORD? Will you forget me forever?
>   How long will you hide your face from me?
> How long must I wrestle with my thoughts
>   and every day have sorrow in my heart?
>   How long will my enemy triumph over me?
> Look on me and answer, O LORD my God.
>   Give light to my eyes, or I will sleep in death;
> my enemy will say, "I have overcome him,"
>   and my foes will rejoice when I fall.
> But I trust in your unfailing love;
>   my heart rejoices in your salvation.
> I will sing to the LORD,
>   for he has been good to me.

This is very short, and it only takes us a few seconds to
read through it. The author complains for four verses and
then utters two verses of assurance. But who knows how many
hours, days, months, or even years it took the psalmist to get
from verse 4 to verse 5? Certainly the first two verses give
the impression that the psalmist has been struggling with his
suffering for a long time. We should also bear in mind that
these psalms were intended to be sung liturgically, not speed-
read silently. The first four verses would have been slowly

repeated, with plenty of time to dwell on the problem of God's silence.

Also note how honest the psalmist is. He is baffled by God's failure to respond and is even so bold as to remind God of his promises. It is as though he said, "You had better come through, God, or my enemies will triumph and you will look bad." But even though he has not yet received a specific answer, he finally reaches the place where he can trust again. It is worth noting how he achieves peace. He remembers God's love, he rejoices in God's salvation, and he remembers how God has been good to him in the past. For the Christian these things are paramount in Jesus. In him we see the perfect outpouring of God's love, in that while we were even sinners in rebellion against God, Christ suffered and died for us. And we see in Jesus God's complete salvation from the hell we had created for ourselves and the hell toward which we were inexorably heading. It is still not easy, and the harder the trial the longer it may take to work through, but the believer can and will eventually again trust God. Where else can the child of God turn?

Psalm 27 is one of the best-loved psalms for its expressions of faith.

> The LORD is my light and my salvation—
>   whom shall I fear?
> The LORD is the stronghold of my life—
>   of whom shall I be afraid?
> When evil men advance against me
>   to devour my flesh,
> when my enemies and my foes attack me,
>   they will stumble and fall.
> Though an army besiege me,
>   my heart will not fear;
> though war break out against me,
>   even then will I be confident.

One thing I ask of the LORD,
  this is what I seek:
that I may dwell in the house of the LORD
  all the days of my life,
to gaze upon the beauty of the LORD
  and to seek him in his temple.
For in the day of trouble
  he will keep me safe in his dwelling;
he will hide me in the shelter of his tabernacle
  and set me high upon a rock.
Then my head will be exalted
  above the enemies who surround me;
at his tabernacle will I sacrifice with shouts of joy;
  I will sing and make music to the LORD.
Hear my voice when I call, O LORD;
  be merciful to me and answer me.
My heart says of you, "Seek his face!"
  Your face, LORD, I will seek.
Do not hide your face from me,
  do not turn your servant away in anger;
  you have been my helper.
Do not reject me or forsake me,
  O God my Savior.
Though my father and mother forsake me,
  the LORD will receive me.
Teach me your way, O LORD;
  lead me in a straight path
  because of my oppressors.
Do not turn me over to the desire of my foes,
  for false witnesses rise up against me,
  breathing out violence.
I am still confident of this:
  I will see the goodness of the LORD
  in the land of the living.

Wait for the LORD;
  be strong and take heart
  and wait for the LORD.

We usually read it as an upbeat, happy psalm, for its great passages: "The LORD is my light and my salvation—whom shall I fear?" and "Wait for the LORD; be strong and take heart and wait for the LORD." But the body of the psalm shows that the psalmist is actually struggling to remain confident. Notice all the terrible things he envisions happening: war on every side, enemies falsely accusing him, his own parents abandoning him, and even God turning away from him. He keeps saying, "I will not be afraid," precisely because fear is lurking very close. He concludes with "Wait for the LORD" because it is hard for him to keep waiting when it already seems so long. Faith is only important when facing difficulty. But when difficulty does come, faith is overwhelmingly important. It is by "seeking God's face," listening for God's voice, expecting his presence, and walking in God's way, that God our light banishes the shadows of fear.

John Calvin said of this psalm, "Certainly we find that all our fears arise from this source, that we are too anxious about our life, while we do not acknowledge that God is its preserver. We can have no tranquillity, therefore, until we attain the persuasion that our life is sufficiently guarded, because it is protected by his omnipotent power. . . ."

Many other psalms testify to the way faith triumphs over fear. That wonderful line in Psalm 23 expresses it well—"even though I must go through the valley of deep shadow, I will fear no evil" (my translation). The line usually translated "the valley of the shadow of death" probably does not convey well enough the darkness that threatens. The verse does not mean simply "even though I have to die . . . ," but rather "even though I must pass through the most intense times of doubt, despair, agony, suffering, and horror, nevertheless I will not fear any of these evils, because you are with me." Some things are even more terrifying than death, but even in these we can, by faith, fear no evil. Even when suffering comes, and even when evil threatens to overwhelm us, the victory of Jesus is secure.

Hope Destroys Hopelessness

Popular wisdom says, "Where there's life there's hope." It might be more accurate to say, "Where there's hope there's life." Hopelessness destroys the will to live, because without hope life is something to be despised. On the other hand, someone who has hope can survive incredible amounts of suffering and frustration.

Hope is sometimes misunderstood. The biblical idea of hope is not the vague kind of wish, as in the expression "I hope so"; it is rather an expectation of relief or deliverance in the future. It is something we hold on to, not when things are going great but precisely when things look bleak. Suffering is the dark background upon which the rays of hope can be shown in their glory. It is the shadow that enhances the light and makes it noticeable. Only the one who has suffered can really know what it is to hope.

One of the great expressions of this kind of hope is *Psalm 22.* Note that the psalm begins by lamenting God's silence and inaction.

> My God, my God, why have you forsaken me?
>   Why are you so far from saving me,
>   so far from the words of my groaning?
> O my God, I cry out by day, but you do not answer,
>   by night, and am not silent. (vv. 1–2)

This is followed by a historical remembrance:

> Yet you are enthroned as the Holy One;
>> you are the praise of Israel.
> In you our fathers put their trust;
>> they trusted and you delivered them.
> They cried to you and were saved;
>> in you they trusted and were not disappointed.
>> (vv. 3–5)

But the psalmist is faced with a "cognitive dissonance," a clash between what he knows from covenant history and what he sees in his experience.

> But I am a worm and not a man,
>> scorned by men and despised by the people.
> All who see me mock me;
>> they hurl insults, shaking their heads:
> "He trusts in the LORD;
>> let the LORD rescue him.
> Let him deliver him,
>> since he delights in him." (vv. 6–8)

But there is also an awareness that God has been personally involved with him as well.

> Yet you brought me out of the womb;
>> you made me trust in you
>> even at my mother's breast.
> From birth I was cast upon you;
>> from my mother's womb you have been my God.
>> (vv. 9–10)

This is followed by the psalmist's most sustained appeal to God to act:

Do not be far from me,
   for trouble is near
   and there is no one to help.
Many bulls surround me;
   strong bulls of Bashan encircle me.
Roaring lions tearing their prey
   open their mouths wide against me.
I am poured out like water,
   and all my bones are out of joint.
My heart has turned to wax;
   it has melted away within me.
My strength is dried up like a potsherd,
   and my tongue sticks to the roof of my mouth;
   you lay me in the dust of death.
Dogs have surrounded me;
   a band of evil men has encircled me,
   they have pierced my hands and my feet.
I can count all my bones;
   people stare and gloat over me.
They divide my garments among them
   and cast lots for my clothing.
But you, O LORD, be not far off;
   O my Strength, come quickly to help me.
Deliver my life from the sword,
   my precious life from the power of the dogs.
Rescue me from the mouth of the lions;
   save me from the horns of the wild oxen. (vv. 11–21)

Thus far, the psalmist has been appealing to God, depicting his distress and begging God to do something. But the psalmist closes with a call to praise God for what he *will* do in the future.

I will declare your name to my brothers;
   in the congregation I will praise you.

You who fear the LORD, praise him!
　　All you descendants of Jacob, honor him!
　　Revere him, all you descendants of Israel!
For he has not despised or disdained
　　the suffering of the afflicted one;
he has not hidden his face from him
　　but has listened to his cry for help.
From you comes the theme of my praise in the great
　　　　assembly;
　　before those who fear you will I fulfill my vows.
The poor will eat and be satisfied;
　　they who seek the LORD will praise him—
　　may your hearts live forever!
All the ends of the earth
　　will remember and turn to the LORD,
and all the families of the nations
　　will bow down before him,
for dominion belongs to the LORD
　　and he rules over the nations.
All the rich of the earth will feast and worship;
　　all who go down to the dust will kneel before
　　　　him—
　　those who cannot keep themselves alive.
Posterity will serve him;
　　future generations will be told about the Lord.
They will proclaim his righteousness
　　to a people yet unborn—
　　for he has done it. (vv. 22–31)

This is not a comfortable psalm. It is a cry of anguish. At times it gets close to despair. But hope for future deliverance, based on what God has done in the past, and especially on his word, prevails and enables the sufferer to overcome.

One of the reasons this psalm is so important is that it is

both quoted by Jesus and applied to Jesus by other New Testament writers. Both Matthew and Mark record that at the apex of his anguish Jesus cried out, "My God, my God, why have you forsaken me?" Jesus cried out "why" to God, just as we do. He was not asking for information; he was uttering his sense of abandonment and loss. If Jesus can express such deep feelings of distress and loss by the words of this psalm, then certainly we who are in Christ can utter the same feelings. Of course, there is a big difference: Jesus really was abandoned by God. We, like the psalmist himself, only feel that way. But the power of the psalm comes in its development and conclusion. Though there is anguish, there is never a loss of hope. Though the present seems indescribably horrible, there is hope, not because we know what will happen, but because God is God and he will restore the world to righteousness. When a conflict occurs between what we see (the present) and what we know (the future), the believer, as hard as it is, keeps returning to that future. The hope that is based on God's word is stronger than any hopelessness and will be vindicated.

A friend of mine had an interesting way of describing how we feel when suffering comes: "I *feel* like I'm inside a machine that is grinding me to bits, while God is standing there feeding quarters into the machine to keep it going. But then it is a question of whether I believe God's word or believe my feelings." The psalmist honestly expressed his feelings, but he also ultimately believed in God's word.

The shift of perspective in verse 22 is especially interesting, because Hebrews 2:12 tells us that Jesus sings with the brethren, quoting this verse. Jesus, Hebrews tells us, needed both to experience suffering and to live in hope as we do. Hope that is seen is not hope; Jesus as a human being had to live by hope in the future promises, not by what he already had (see Heb. 12:2). This is the same spot we are in. This is why Peter says Jesus left us an example of how to suffer. We suffer, as Jesus did, and we pray about it the way he did, by the Psalms.

In **Psalm 42** the psalmist is so depressed over his suffering and feelings of abandonment that he must adjure himself to maintain his attitude of hope. Note especially the refrain in verses 5 and 11, "Put your hope in God."

> As the deer pants for streams of water,
>   so my soul pants for you, O God.
> My soul thirsts for God, for the living God.
>   When can I go and meet with God?
> My tears have been my food
>   day and night,
> while men say to me all day long,
>   "Where is your God?"
> These things I remember
>   as I pour out my soul:
> how I used to go with the multitude,
>   leading the procession to the house of God,
> with shouts of joy and thanksgiving
>   among the festive throng.
> Why are you downcast, O my soul?
>   Why so disturbed within me?
> Put your hope in God,
>   for I will yet praise him,
>   my Savior and my God.
> My soul is downcast within me;
>   therefore I will remember you
> from the land of the Jordan,
>   the heights of Hermon—from Mount Mizar.
> Deep calls to deep
>   in the roar of your waterfalls;
> all your waves and breakers
>   have swept over me.

By day the LORD directs his love,
 at night his song is with me—
 a prayer to the God of my life.
I say to God my Rock,
 "Why have you forgotten me?
Why must I go about mourning,
 oppressed by the enemy?"
My bones suffer mortal agony
 as my foes taunt me,
saying to me all day long,
 "Where is your God?"
Why are you downcast, O my soul?
 Why so disturbed within me?
Put your hope in God,
 for I will yet praise him,
 my Savior and my God.

One of the reasons suffering is so devastating is that it produces *mental* anguish. We become tremendously depressed when God allows us to suffer. For one thing, the very fact that we are suffering raises severe doubts as to whether God loves us. And it certainly makes God seem very remote. The author of Psalm 42 clearly feels this. He yearns for God's reassuring presence.

Once again, note how the psalmist looks to the future. Even though the psalmist is too depressed to praise God now, he knows he will be able to do so in the future, because he knows God will deliver him. It is as though what he knows by faith (God cares for him) is struggling with what he sees happening. Note how verses 8 and 9 are at odds.

 8By day the LORD directs his love,
  at night his song is with me—
  a prayer to the God of my life.

⁹I say to God my Rock,
   "Why have you forgotten me?
Why must I go about mourning,
   oppressed by the enemy?"

But hope wins! The psalmist *remembers* God's faithfulness, as a means of dealing with his depression and suffering: "My soul is downcast within me; therefore I will remember you. . . ." Psalm 34:19 (another psalm applied to Jesus) says, "A righteous man may have many troubles, but the LORD delivers him from them all." Hence, even though his praise is future, it is also now. Without hope, there could be no trust, no praising of God; but true hope makes the future reality a present reality.

Love Banishes Loneliness

Love means different things to different people, but God's love means, at least, that he does not leave his loved ones alone. I do not mean that he never relents from sanctifying us, although that too is true, but that he does not leave us lonely.

Sufferers yearn for companionship. This is something else I learned from my bout with kidney stones. When I was lying on the gurney in the hospital, my colleague came and sat with me. He had brought a book, and he just sat and read his book. I did not want to talk. I did not want him to talk. But I greatly appreciated his just being there reading his book. But sometimes we find ourselves in places where no one comes and sits with us. It is then that we most need to remember that God is there with us, identifying with us in our suffering.

Although the New Testament is much clearer on this because we see how God himself experienced our suffering, we

can also see in the Psalms how God's love for us and our love
for God overcomes the anguish of the loneliness of suffering.

An excellent example of this is **Psalm 73.** This psalm is
dealing with the problem of why the righteous seem to suffer
much more than the wicked. The prosperity of the wicked
and the misery of the righteous are threatening to under-
mine the psalmist's faith in God. But love is what gets things
into perspective.

It certainly does seem as if the wicked suffer *less* and the
righteous suffer more. The Bible lists several reasons why this
is actually so. First, we have seen that God disciplines those
he loves. Second, if the world hated Jesus, it will also hate
his brothers and sisters. Third, Satan is especially diligent in
afflicting the righteous, as happened to Job. Finally, Christians are much more torn by the internal battle against sin;
in the Christian, the old sinful nature wars against the new
righteous nature, and this can have its outworking in external situations as well. Still, it just seems to go against the
moral order that we see wicked people prospering and the
godly suffering, and this can lead to envy as well as confusion. The psalmist is very honest about this:

> For I envied the arrogant
> when I saw the prosperity of the wicked.
> They have no struggles;
> their bodies are healthy and strong.
> They are free from the burdens common to man;
> they are not plagued by human ills.
> Therefore pride is their necklace;
> they clothe themselves with violence.
> From their callous hearts comes iniquity;
> the evil conceits of their minds know no limits.
> They scoff, and speak with malice;
> in their arrogance they threaten oppression.

Their mouths lay claim to heaven,
and their tongues take possession of the earth.
Therefore their people turn to them
and drink up waters in abundance.
They say, "How can God know?
Does the Most High have knowledge?"
This is what the wicked are like—
always carefree, they increase in wealth. (vv. 3–12)

On the other hand, the psalmist only receives pain and tribulation for his righteousness:

Surely in vain have I kept my heart pure;
in vain have I washed my hands in innocence.
All day long I have been plagued;
I have been punished every morning. (vv. 13–14)

Yet the psalmist does not stay focused on present appearances. He also knows there is a future. Note the turning point in verse 17.

If I had said, "I will speak thus,"
I would have betrayed your children.
When I tried to understand all this,
it was oppressive to me
till I entered the sanctuary of God;
then I understood their final destiny.
Surely you place them on slippery ground;
you cast them down to ruin.
How suddenly are they destroyed,
completely swept away by terrors!
As a dream when one awakes,
so when you arise, O Lord,
you will despise them as fantasies. (vv. 15–20)

It was by coming back into God's presence that the psalmist was reminded of the true situation. Apart from God's presence is meaninglessness and brutishness:

> When my heart was grieved
>   and my spirit embittered,
> I was senseless and ignorant;
>   I was a brute beast before you. (vv. 21–22)

But God's love is not dependent on us, and when we realize that God himself is our portion, we no longer need to
have an answer to every question:

> Yet I am always with you;
>   you hold me by my right hand.
> You guide me with your counsel,
>   and afterward you will take me into glory.
> Whom have I in heaven but you?
>   And earth has nothing I desire besides you.
> My flesh and my heart may fail,
>   but God is the strength of my heart
>   and my portion forever.
> Those who are far from you will perish;
>   you destroy all who are unfaithful to you.
> But as for me, it is good to be near God.
>   I have made the Sovereign LORD my refuge;
>   I will tell of all your deeds. (vv. 23–28)

The psalmist does not actually see the punishment of the
wicked and the restoration of the righteous. He only per-
ceives what the *future* holds. His hope is restored by recall-
ing his first love. Ultimately it was God's love for the
psalmist, which in turn evoked his love for God, that pre-
vailed. If God holds your hand, you cannot be alone. If

God is your counselor, you are never without an advisor and comforter.

Rich folks like to talk about their "net worth." But true value comes not from financial assets or real estate but from relationships. If you have a deep and certain relationship with an infinite God then your "net worth" is infinite. To put it in the psalmist's terms, if God is our portion, our inheritance, what need have we of any temporary, earthly thing? Thus, for this struggling soul, it is good just to be near God. But remember that the writer of this psalm did not easily come to the point of his delighting purely in the presence of God. It was a great struggle. Who knows how long it took before this writer could in fact "enter the sanctuary of God"?

Remember how despairing the disciples of Jesus were after his crucifixion? It certainly looked like the wicked had won not just the battle but the whole war. Yet Mary Magdalene, out of *love* for Jesus, came to the tomb on Jesus' resurrection day, just to be with his remains. Love will prevail even when faith and hope shrivel. Mary no doubt felt confused and hope-less, so much so that she could not at first recognize Jesus. But she never stopped loving him. She had the attitude ex-pressed in another psalm that shows how love overcomes suffering, namely Psalm 131.

Psalm 131 is a very brief poem, but is exactly to the point.

> My heart is not proud, O LORD,
>   my eyes are not haughty;
> I do not concern myself with great matters
>   or things too wonderful for me.
> But I have stilled and quieted my soul;
>   like a weaned child with his mother,
>   like a weaned child is my soul within me.
> O Israel, put your hope in the LORD
>   both now and forevermore.

How do you deal with the times when God is silent? The psalmist acknowledges that he cannot know the details of God's plan, because there are some things that God has not revealed. But nevertheless, he stills and quiets his soul, like a weaned child with his mother—not like a baby, who knows only warmth and food, but like a *weaned* child, a child who knows and completely trusts his mother and does not worry about what his mother is doing. To some degree, the "why" of suffering will always be a "great matter and a thing too wonderful for us." God help us become like little children such as this, for to such, says Jesus, the kingdom of heaven belongs.

For Further Consideration

1. If you have experienced suffering, did fear play any part in compounding it? What about loneliness and hopelessness?

2. How can we help other sufferers deal with fear, hopelessness, and loneliness?

3. Do you have a favorite psalm? Does it deal in some way with suffering? What other psalms have you found very helpful in dealing with suffering?

4. In many psalms dealing with suffering, the future and God's promises about the future figure very prominently. Why is the future so important to the believer in dealing with suffering? Why is the past important?

5. In the book of Ruth, Naomi renames herself "Bitter" because God has taken away her fullness and given her emptiness. How would you comfort someone like Naomi who is struggling with bitterness?

6. Some people propound the "power of positive thinking" as a means of handling suffering in their lives. How is the biblical answer similar to and different from the "power of positive thinking"?

NOTES

1. *Where Is God When It Hurts* (New York: Harper, 1977), 149–58.
2. Shakespeare, *King Lear*, Act 4, Scene 7.

Taking God at His Word

JESUS TOLD HIS DISCIPLES, "Take my yoke upon you and learn from me, for I am gentle and humble in heart, and you will find rest for your souls. For my yoke is easy and my burden is light" (Matt. 11:29–30). The problem is, the yoke does not always look very easy. We sometimes see it as a crushing burden. But remember what a yoke does—it connects *two* oxen to the plow. If you are connected to Jesus' yoke, then with whom are you being yoked? Who is doing the real pulling? Being yoked together with Jesus means we share in his sufferings—and he shares in ours. He shared in our corrupt and corruptible flesh. We share in his resurrection and glorification. Who is getting the better deal? If you refuse his yoke, which will include suffering in this life, what is the alternative? Although his yoke may seem grievous at times, it is exceedingly easy and light compared to bearing a yoke all by ourselves. If suffering yokes me with Jesus, I am willing, Lord.

Thus can we say with the psalmist when God sends suffering: "in faithfulness you have afflicted me" (Ps. 119:75).

The Mystery of Providence

When we experience suffering, we frequently have to say we do not know why God should allow it. Sometimes (not always) we may later find out a reason for that particular suffering and be able to see God's providence in it, but the answer to suffering while it is happening can often be no more than "hang on!" with the assurance from Romans 8:28 that God's providence is *always* at work, even though we do not perceive it at the moment. This is not always very easy to accept. But neither is it a "leap of faith" that simply flies in the face of all evidence. Above all there is the testimonial of the suffering of Jesus, which gives our suffering focus and perspective. But we also sometimes see both in our own lives and in Scripture the evidence that suffering does have a good purpose.

Perhaps we can learn something from Jacob's experience. In Genesis 42:36, Jacob in the midst of his considerable troubles cries out, "Everything is against me." It certainly looked to Jacob as if his life could hardly get any more miserable. His family was starving, his beloved son Joseph was dead (he thought), Simeon was gone, a hostile Egyptian ruler was demanding that his other dearest son Benjamin go to Egypt as the price of more food, and probably the whole family was branded as thieves and faced the choice of either imprisonment and possibly death in Egypt or starvation in Palestine. But actually, God was making amazing provision for that family. Joseph was in fact not dead but the second-ranked person in Egypt, who intended not to throw them in prison but to rescue and honor the entire family.

Often, indeed usually, we do not see the whole picture, and God appears to be doing things that to us look not at all helpful. We may be tempted to cry out "Everything is against me" at the very times that God is being most generous and providential. How often have you asked God "Don't you care?!" When the disciples in the boat asked Jesus that (Mark 4:38), he responded, "Are you still without faith?!" But Jesus did indeed calm the storm.

In dealing with your suffering or with the suffering of those around you, do not minimize the importance of God's word. In Psalm 119:92 David says, "If your law [your instruction] had not been my delight, I would have perished in my affliction." When God sends suffering, your feelings will be strong that God has abandoned you, that he is abusing you, and that the suffering is utterly incomprehensible. It is only by reflection on God's word that you will be able to get everything into perspective. I encourage you to do that *before* your crisis comes.

For Further Consideration

1. Why did Jesus use the image of a yoke to describe discipleship?
2. What are some of the mysteries of your life? How are you handling them?
3. Have you ever thought that everything was against you? Describe what made you feel that way. If you do not still feel that way, why not?
4. What is the difference between genuine trust in God even when he appears to be against us, and a "leap of faith"?
5. What aspects of suffering in your own life did this book fail to address? Does the Bible address them? Explain.

APPENDIX

Some Bible Passages on Suffering

THE BIBLE IS FULL of passages dealing with suffering, and the following list is by no means exhaustive. But these are some good passages to study in your quest to understand what suffering means, and how God uses it in our lives.

Genesis 37, 39–50. A story of redemptive suffering. How God used the suffering of one man (Joseph) to remedy the suffering of an entire family.

Exodus 1–20. How God delivered his people from great suffering by defeating their oppressors.

Numbers 13–14. Suffering because of sin. How the Israelites rebelled against God and as a result were made homeless refugees for an entire generation.

Joshua 7:1–5. A whole nation suffers because one individual sinned.

Ruth. How God brought bitterness and emptiness but then turned that bitterness to joy. We also see here how the faithfulness and love of a mother-in-law and daughter-in-law enabled them to deal with their suffering until God brought deliverance.

1 Samuel 18–31. A story about how a man who deeply trusts in God (David) suffers many years of persecution and exile because of that trust.

1 & 2 Kings. A long, sad story about how many years of increasing unfaithfulness, punctuated now and again by a few faithful individuals, led to a harsh punishment inflicted on an entire people.

Job. There is a great deal of insight into the nature and meaning of unjustified suffering in the book of Job that we could not cover in this book. This is well worth studying closely.

Psalms. As noted in chapter 9, there are many, many psalms that deal with suffering. And many more that are not directly concerned with suffering nevertheless have the experience of suffering in the background. Insight into many of the psalms can be gained simply by asking the question, "How was the author's experience of past or present or threatened future suffering related to what he says in this psalm?" Here are some of the psalms most directly concerned with suffering: 4–7; 10–13; 22; 25; 28; 42–43; 55–57; 59–60; 64; 69–70; 74; 77; 79; 86; 88; 102; 123; 130; 137; 140–43.

Isaiah 53. The great prophecy of the Servant of the Lord who was to suffer redemptively for the people of God.

Jeremiah 38. A godly man suffers for speaking the truth about God.

Lamentations. Jeremiah's very personal expression of sadness, agony, and yet hope as the people of God suffer punishment for their sin.

Jonah. A reluctant prophet suffers so that he might learn the character of God.

Matthew 26–27; Mark 14–15; Luke 22–23; John 18–19. It may seem obvious, but the story of Jesus' suffering has many lessons for the sufferer that are sometimes overlooked. Jesus experienced persecution from his own people, betrayal by one of his close associates, abandonment by his friends, physical torture, mockery and humiliation, abandonment by God and the consequent experience of hell—in short, just about every kind of suffering possible. If Jesus is our example of how to suffer (1 Peter 2:21), we should pay attention to it.

Acts 21–28. An account of some of Paul's suffering for the sake of the gospel.

Philippians 1:12–30. Paul's confidence that his suffering has a good purpose, some of which he can already see.

1 Thessalonians. Suffering was the context of people coming to faith, the context of their continued believing, and the dynamic that caused them to focus on the future promise of God's coming in judgment.

Hebrews 4:14–5:10. An exposition of how Christ's suffering in the Garden of Gethsemane prior to his execution enables him to be sympathetic with us.

Hebrews 12. God disciplines his children.

1 Peter. As noted earlier, this letter is almost entirely concerned with the meaning of Christian suffering. First Peter is very complex and never stops yielding insights to those willing to study it.

Revelation. Many Christians are wary of this book because it sounds so weird. Others use it to try to "figure out" the future, by assigning some specific meaning to every symbol. But the main message of the book is addressed to people enduring suffering, encouraging them by reminding them that God's sovereign purpose is behind the suffering and he will bring it all to a satisfactory conclusion.